FEAST OF JOY

FEAST OF JOY

Pat

Patricia Carver Knight

XULON PRESS

Xulon Press
2301 Lucien Way #415
Maitland, FL 32751
407.339.4217
www.xulonpress.com

Printed in the United States of America.

ISBN-13: 978-1-6305-0413-7

TABLE OF CONTENTS

TABLE OF CONTENTS

FOREWORD

P at Knight and I have been friends for more than fifty years. We were first introduced when my future wife, Cathy, and Pat, were roommates at college. We participated in each other's weddings and we've consistently prayed for family members during many challenges we encountered throughout the ensuing decades.

Later when we visited, we relished the joyful immediacy of the friendship we had missed due to the geographical distance between us. Rediscovery was always filled with delight. Pat is a joy-filled, hopeful encourager, so during our special visits she engaged us in conversation that emphasized Jesus' interactions with His believers, and the miraculous responses we witnessed to our earnest intercessions. We all agreed that no one is inconsequential in the Lord's plans. He takes great joy in implementing seemingly small situations and insignificant people to authenticate His kingdom, power, and glory.

Pat seeks the peace of mind Christ lavishes in a believer's life through all circumstances. *FEAST of JOY* is an apt title for a book penned by Pat, an advocate for spiritual exuberance and contagious rejoicing personified by the Son of God.

When Cathy and I were vacationing in Acadia National Park in 2006, our leisurely bicycle trip ended abruptly when Cathy veered off the trail, struck a tree, and was flung backward onto a sheet of granite. Air-lifted to a trauma center, she was diagnosed with a spinal cord injury. Pat and Roger were the first visitors at the ICU, traveling hours to respond to my call. They shared our shock and grief, followed by Pat's encouragement, reminding us of God's comfort and love, assuring us that He would not leave us in desperation. Though at the time we had no immediate answers, we were all convinced God would work His perfect plan to bring glory to His sovereign name and purpose. Our heavenly Father is faithful; He never disappoints!

Pat immediately began a personal handwritten letter campaign that coordinated with Cathy's rehabilitation and recovery efforts, ultimately sending weekly notes of encouraging correspondence to her dear friend for the next eight years.

The devotionals contained in *FEAST of JOY* remind me that Jesus comes alongside to shower us with His strength, regardless of our circumstances. The apostle Paul captured Jesus' method of blessing his life centuries ago, the same promise currently offered to us: *"' My grace is sufficient for you, for my power is made perfect in weakness'" (2 Corinthians 12:9).*

Joy is also a gift from God, independent of our circumstances, buoying each of us during our spiritual journey. The feast of joy to which the author draws our attention is the pleasure of experiencing God's grace in every moment, exceeding any amount of hardship. Our Lord alone possesses the power to accomplish His objectives with boundless love and mercy in the midst of our trials.

Opening these pages, I hope you will prepare for a feast, an epicurean journey for the senses: sight, smell, taste, touch; even hearing, as you are reminded of the Israelite's songs of praise in the Old and New Testaments of God's Word. To enjoy a feast, you must be in the moment, as all stimuli bombard nerve receptors, minimizing the past, not yet focusing on the future, but setting goals to feast on the current moment of joy and riches emanating from their infinite source.

My prayer for readers of the enclosed devotionals: enjoy the *FEAST of JOY* spread before you. Return for multiple servings!

Kenneth Campbell, DMin
Pastor Emeritus, Emmanuel Presbyterian Church (PCA)
Cedar Park, TX

PREFACE

In the following pages, I invite you to join me in plumbing the depths of God's understanding, wisdom, and splendor. As designer, engineer, and creator of the entire universe, all power and authority reside in Him. We begin to comprehend our working relationship with the King of kings and Lord of lords as God speaks to us through the inspired dialogue of His Word. Jesus, the provider of all of our needs, is Living Water, Bread of Life, and our Great Shepherd. God is the self-identified great I AM, the exclusive, unchanging, self-existing deity, who is actively present in His children's lives. Our Lord is infinite, unlimited by time or space. His characteristics of righteousness, purity, and compassion are extended to believers through Jesus Christ, the living Savior, who died a humiliating, heinous crucifixion to redeem our sins. Then, He arose from the dead to secure eternal life for His followers.

God's love is immeasurably greater than any relationship we experience on earth. His power exceeds that of an atomic bomb or a rocket thrust into space. He counts the stars in the cosmos, calling each by name, just as He numbers the hair on our heads. He is the everlasting embodiment of supremacy and sovereignty, empowering His creation with unlimited strength and protection. We serve a personal God, who invites us to fellowship with Him; His love and grace overcome human frailties. Our faint call assures His undivided attention, followed by blessings aplenty. Expect the unexpected from the exceptional, eternal, heavenly Father.

A joyous spirit is our spontaneous response to the magnificent, monumental love with which our Lord lavishes believers. Joy reduces disappointment, anger, and fear, reserving quality heart space for ecstasy. It is my hope and prayer that each day you will awaken to participate in a spectacular spiritual extravaganza of joy, demonstrating the resplendent glory and majesty of the Lord.

God commands that we rejoice always. Joy is not manufactured. It is a heaven-sent gift; an inner exuberance; a constant dimension of a believer's life. As you partake from the *FEAST OF JOY* spread before you, may you acquire new appreciation for God's desire to fill your heart to the brim with Him.

We are intended to perpetuate joy wherever we go, to whomever we meet, revealing exhilarating outward evidence of the indwelling Savior. Like a raging communicable disease, let us impact the world with God's overwhelming gift of joy, guided by King David's proc-lamation: *"'My heart leaps for joy and with my song I praise Him'"* *(Psalm 28:7).*

—Pat Knight

A FEAST OF JOY

J oy is a perpetual, delicious smorgasbord of delight, an avalanche of dazzling possibilities encompassing the heart and
mind. Joy is exhilarating, lavishing us with zeal. Joy is an abundant,
delectable banquet of life. *"The cheerful heart has a continual
feast" (Proverbs 15:15b)*. Joy captivates behavior and engages our
senses, conveying joy-filled emotions with sparkling eyes, a wide
smile, or effervescent verbal expressions.

The exchange of wedding vows amplifies hearts in love, engulfing
the husband and wife with radiance and rejoicing. In such instances,
joy owns the gamut of our emotions, rendering us incapable of
managing surges of exhilaration. Our hearts stagger under the load,
as if our epicenter of joy spontaneously implodes.

The psalmist, David, jubilantly expressed, *"'My heart is glad and
my tongue rejoices ... You will fill me with joy in your presence,
with eternal pleasures at your right hand'" (Psalm 16: 9, 11)*.
God's Word is replete with examples of people whose joy knew
no bounds, even under the most profoundly challenging circumstances. Miriam, sister of Moses, unabashedly rallied the Hebrew
women to sing, using tambourines and dance to passionately

express joy and gratitude to their Lord following His miraculous delivery of the nation of Israel from centuries of slavery in Egypt. The women converted their sorrow and mourning into enthusiastic praise to God for His spectacular victory over the Egyptian pharaoh and militia.

King David was ecstatic that the ark of the covenant, the representation of God's throne on earth, was returned to Israelite territory. The Philistines had captured it decades before, considering it no more than a lucky talisman. Rallying the people in a Jerusalem street parade, *"David was dancing before the Lord with all his might, while he and all Israel were bringing up the ark of the Lord with shouts and the sound of trumpets" (2 Samuel 6:14-15)*. It was a time of tremendous rejoicing of national impact. David's dance was one of true worship, demonstrating irrepressible love for his Lord.

Paul and Silas were captured by the Roman authorities, then stripped and beaten. Once severely flogged with a whip, they were thrown into an inner cell in a dark, malodorous prison with their feet fastened in stocks. *"About midnight Paul and Silas were praying and singing hymns to God, and the other prisoners were listening to them" (Acts 16:25)*. Suddenly a violent earthquake shook the prison foundation, opening the cell doors and loosening prisoners' chains. The jailer, responsible for all prisoners, was startled from sleep, and assumed the prisoners had escaped. Paul and Silas intervened before the jailor committed suicide with his sword. Then the guard requested that the missionaries present the Gospel to him and his family. The jailer was *"filled with joy because he had come to believe in God—he and his whole family" (Acts 16:34)*.

What unusual events were set in motion by God, who was honored and worshipped in the midst of life-threatening conditions! When we trust the Almighty, joy prevails supreme, regardless of adverse situations.

Jesus began the Sermon on the Mount by listing eight beatitudes, or blessings, promising unprecedented joy for the inner person. The Messiah announced an upside-down kingdom where believers assimilate His attributes of humility, justice, righteousness; comfort for the grieving, victory for the meek, and mercy for those who suffer.

The pursuit of blessedness is fullness of joy in God's presence (Psalm 16:11). Throughout His life, Jesus espoused abundant joy, lavishing purity, peace, and righteousness on His followers. Ideal disciples are those who exhibit the characteristics of the Son of God. Believers partake of a perpetual feast, wholeheartedly accepting generous portions of Christ's gifts of Living Water and the Bread of Life.

Jesus Christ is the epitome of joy. He who was sinless during his entire life on earth, acknowledged His ultimate mission was to glorify His Father by offering His life as the perfect sacrifice to redeem sinners. The peace Jesus revealed during his brutal trial and agonizing crucifixion is beyond our finite understanding. Though Jesus was exhausted and suffering on all levels, He rejoiced spiritually, accomplishing the purpose for which He relinquished His glory in heaven for a season to live on earth: to offer Himself as the perfect sacrificial Lamb to atone for the sins of humanity.

If Jesus could prompt any amount of joy while confronting a terrifying, heinous crucifixion, it was only because He spent quality time with His heavenly Father in prayer, who strengthened Jesus' commitment to His task on earth. Utter joy is only possible for us because through Jesus' death and resurrection, He guarantees our inheritance, providing a glorious eternity in heaven.

When Jesus appeared to His followers on Resurrection Sunday, He revealed the crucifixion wounds in His hands and torso. The disciples were so ecstatic to see Jesus alive, their joy was contagious, extending throughout centuries to our current generation. *"Though you have not seen him, you love him; and even though you do not see him now, you believe in him and are filled with an inexpressible and glorious joy" (1 Peter 1:8).* The Apostle Paul, though frequently a victim of unjustified hostility and extreme suffering, admonished believers: *"'Rejoice in the Lord always. I will say it again: Rejoice!'" (Philippians 4:4).* Indeed, the command to rejoice is repeated, emphasizing its importance. Christ was the source and secret of Paul's joy, illustrating that the suffering and security of believers produces unmitigated rejoicing.

One of life's objectives is irrefutable: worshipful joy in which God's entire creation participates. *"Let the heavens rejoice, let the earth be glad; let the sea resound, and all that is in it. Let the fields be jubilant, and everything in them; let all the trees of the forest sing for joy" (Psalm 96:11-12).* Joy is splendiferous, manifesting praise and thanksgiving! *"Clap your hands, all you nations; shout to God with cries of joy. For the Lord Most High is awesome, the great King over all the earth" (Psalm 47:1-2).* Let us saturate our world with bountiful joy.

STORMS OF LIFE

The sky was camouflaged with black blankets of foreboding storm clouds warning of impending turmoil over coastal waters. So defeated were the roiling, crashing ocean waves that the raucous calls of seabirds were subdued. The wind hushed. Shoreline trees stood at focused attention, awaiting maritime signals. Undeniable calm and quiet prevailed. Surely a gargantuan storm threatened to eviscerate the tightly sutured clouds with scintillating bolts of lightning.

Then mysteriously, tiny holes of blue peeped through the ominous yellow-black thunderheads. The potential pandemonium lessened with every fragment of light escaping. Without a crack of thunder or a drop of rain, fissures of blue sky opened, exposing beautifully clear firmament. "Caw, caw" identified the previously mute avian life.

In time, the entire convulsive pattern of the atmosphere reconfigured, with puffy cotton ball clouds bouncing on a cerulean blue trampoline sky. All appearances and activities normalized as if no threats once loomed. Mischievous clouds would hover over the vast ocean waters again, but not today.

There are times when intimidating clouds stall precariously over our lives, converting our positive focus into negative attitudes. Fear and anxiety rule our decision-making. Frustration and anger claim precedence. When we are threatened by a situation beyond our control, the approaching dismal storm paralyzes our mental reactions, convincing us of the worst possible outcome. Ineptness overwhelms and fear disables, forcing us to merely hunker down until the storm clouds pass. *"Have no fear of sudden disaster or of the ruin that overtakes the wicked, for the Lord will be at your side and will keep your foot from being snared" (Proverbs 3:25-26).*

Joseph was born in Jacob's old age. His father's preferential treatment of Joseph, accentuated by Jacob's gift of a richly ornamental coat, compounded his brothers' insane jealousy of their youngest sibling. When Joseph's dreams revealed that his brothers would eventually bow down to worship him, animosity grew exponentially.

Joseph was seventeen years old when his brothers plotted to kill him (Genesis 37:19). Instead, they stripped him of his multi-colored coat and threw him into an empty well. When Midianite traders passed by, the brothers seized the opportunity to sell Joseph as a slave. Potiphar, the captain of the guard for the Egyptian king, purchased him for palace duty for twenty shekels of silver. *"From the day Joseph was put in charge of his master's household and property, the Lord began to bless Potiphar's household for Joseph's sake" (Genesis 39:5, NLT).*

One day Joseph was accused of a crime he didn't commit. Into prison Joseph went for two long years, seemingly forgotten. Even while confined in jail, God protected His faithful servant, advancing

Joseph to a position of leadership over his fellow prisoners. Such tragedies as Joseph experienced in his young life might tend to destroy a weaker man's faith, but Joseph's spiritual strength grew as he learned to depend upon God for all of his needs. *"Even the very hairs of your head are all numbered" (Matthew 10:30).* Surely, if our Lord makes it His priority to know such intimate details about His children, we are assured that He loves us, cares for us, and that He is constantly working in our lives to accomplish His purpose.

The Egyptian king, warned in a dream that seven years of agricultural plenty would precede seven years of famine, chose Joseph to collect grain supplies during the seven years of abundance. Joseph then approved the sale of grain to Egypt's starving neighbors as famine ravaged the known world, leading to a reunion and reconciliation with his siblings, who had planned his demise twenty years earlier. Though Joseph had suffered injustice and humiliation, he didn't harbor bitterness toward his brothers. His faith was firmly planted in God, who guided his entire life. *"The Lord comforts his people and will have compassion on his afflicted ones" (Isaiah 49:13b).*

Joseph forgave his brothers, revealing his identity to them through tears of joy. *"'I am your brother Joseph, the one you sold into Egypt! And now, do not be distressed and do not be angry with yourselves for selling me here, because it was to save lives that God sent me ahead of you … to preserve for you a remnant on earth and to save your lives by a great deliverance'" (Genesis 45:4b-5, 7).* Though we may neither anticipate nor understand God's exalted plans, we are assured that His intent is always for our benefit and His glorification.

Does adversity create mental chaos and meltdowns in your life? Suffering affliction can either turn our thoughts upward toward God or inward toward self-pity. *"'Because he loves me' says the Lord, 'I will rescue him; I will protect him, for he acknowledges my name. He will call on me, and I will answer him; I will be with him in trouble. I will deliver him and honor him. With long life will I satisfy him and show him my salvation'" (Psalm 91:14-16).*

Like Joseph, let us depend upon God, who has kept every one of His promises from the beginning of time. Faith is not based on ragged emotions borne on desperation, but on trust and confidence. God loves us so immensely, He sent His only Son to die to forgive our multitude of sins. Likewise, Joseph forgave his brothers for the inhumane act that surely would have led to a slow, agonizing death had God not converted the injustice to His purpose.

The initial clamor of the atmospheric storm over the ocean created fear and havoc, but gradually the anticipation of a full-fledged storm system was replaced with tranquility. How many storms in our lives begin with boisterous, threatening circumstances, but as we rest in God's will, He works out the details perfectly, calming our spirits, and reversing the impending situation? When we trust our fears to Jesus, we routinely experience blue skies of peace lingering on the horizon of our emotions. Our perspective is modified as we view life through the lens of Almighty God.

Take Jesus on every excursion of your life. He is the only one in whom to solidly place your trust for all of the big and little problems that assail. *"He guards the paths of the just and protects those who are faithful to him" (Proverbs 2:8, NLT).*

COMPLEX CREATIVIY

L est we fail to recognize that all of God's creations are spectacular, consider the amazing complexity of the pitcher plant. It is named to reflect modified leaves rolled to resemble a container such as a slender pitcher, which functions on the basis of deception. Indigenous to marshy forests of the American continent, the pitcher plant is carnivorous, possessing a mechanism called a pitfall trap. The trap is a deep cavity at the bottom of the pitcher filled with digestive fluid. Insects are attracted to the plant's abyss by visual lures or fragrance. The rim of the pitcher plant is wet and slippery, seducing prey into the trap. The one-way hazardous pit is assisted by downward growing hairs or waxy scales on the interior of the plant to prevent escape. Fluid inside the pitcher plant drowns and dissolves insects, converting them into nutrients.

How many pitcher plants have we encountered in our personal lives? Disappointment, disillusionment, and discouragement are all adept at entrapping us. If we aren't diligent, those same lures are capable of engulfing us with negative attitudes that, over time, drown our hope and dissolve our faith, leaving us no escape from danger or strife.

Satan is a spiritual pitcher plant. Like the aroma and color that attracts insects, *"Satan himself masquerades as an angel of light" (2 Corinthians 11:14),* though his nature is one of evil and darkness. Satan isn't the red-horned monster wielding a pitchfork, as frequently depicted in cartoons. He always appears as something pleasing and captivating, making temptation attractive and irresistible. Whenever Satan appears, he is stunningly beautiful and charming.

It is Satan's purpose to rob us of joy and fellowship with our heavenly Father. He exploits God's gifts by misrepresenting them. Reflect on his cunning methods of enticing Eve in the Garden of Eden, misquoting God's words to suit his purposes. Satan, the epitome of sin and darkness, hates mankind. He is evil to the core, not possessing one good intention.

Don't be a victimized by Satan's manipulative gimmicks. Claim the victory Almighty God offers. *"Submit yourself, then, to God. Resist the devil, and he will flee from you. Come near to God and he will come near to you" (James 4:7-8).* By seeking God's powerful intervention, we gain protection from Satan's evil intrusion into our lives.

God is a gentleman; He never cajoles or begs. He waits patiently for us to call on His name. When invited, our Lord immediately responds with forgiveness of transgressions, surrounding us with love and grace. We need only accept His free gift of salvation for release of bondage to sin.

The devil is the enemy of every believer. Each Christian is engaged in spiritual warfare against Satan and his minions. Our Lord doesn't expect us to fight Satan singlehandedly, for our strength is inadequate; God's power is undefeatable. We are urged to stand firmly as our Lord defends us. *"Be prepared. You're up against far more than you can handle on your own. Take all the help you can get, every weapon God has issued ... Truth, righteousness, peace, faith, and salvation are more than words. Learn how to apply them. You'll need them throughout your life. God's Word is an indispensable weapon. In the same way, prayer is essential in this ongoing warfare. Pray hard and long." (Ephesians 6:13-18, The Msg.).*

In spiritual battles, God provides two weapons to assure victory: the Word of God and prayer with God. Jesus quoted God's Word as His defense against Satan's methods when He was tempted in the wilderness. The Word of God is also referred to as the sword of the Spirit. *"For the word of God is alive and powerful. It is sharper than the sharpest two-edged sword, cutting between soul and spirit, between joint and marrow. It exposes our innermost thoughts and desires. Nothing in all creation is hidden from God. Everything is naked and exposed before his eyes, and he is the one to whom we are accountable" (Hebrews 4:12-13, NLT).* The dynamic Word of God is active in fulfilling God's plans. Satan absolutely fears God the Father and God the Son, and he trembles at their words. Therefore, scripture memory equips us with recollection of God's words, valuable defensive weapons when we are engaged in spiritual warfare.

By immersing our thoughts in God's Word, we learn His assurances of love and grace, which our Lord delights in lavishing upon

His children. He opens our hearts to knowledge and wisdom. Familiarity with God's Word implants understanding of our heavenly Father within our hearts, motivating us to respond with obedience and submission to His sovereign will.

Our other armament against Satan is prayer. If on earth we desire to know people more fully, we spend time communicating with them. The same holds true with God. Not only do we talk, but we also listen, as God directs us into His paths of righteousness. By harkening to God, by trusting and following Him, believers triumph when confronted with seemingly impossible obstacles.

Jesus, the perfect Lamb, offered His one holy life to redeem the sins of those who humbly request His forgiveness. Due to Christ's grace, God now looks at us through Jesus' characteristic of righteousness. We still face temptation, as Jesus did when He walked this earth, but temptation leads to sin only when we yield to Satan's enticements.

The consequence of pulling away from a close walk with Jesus is that we are much more susceptible to Satan's devious, nefarious purposes. Like the pitcher plant, Satan's methods are crafty and slippery. Before we realize it, we have succumbed to his wily ways, dissolved in bitterness and anger, drowned in hate, and digested in evil.

"Let us then approach God's throne of grace with confidence, so that we may receive mercy and find grace to help us in our time of need" (Hebrews 4:16). We are confident Jesus not only understands our weaknesses, but He also supplies us with His supreme, sympathetic solutions as He surrounds us with his lovingkindness.

PATIENCE

The Bible book of Job opens with a snapshot of its namesake: *"In the land of Uz, there lived a man whose name was Job. This man was blameless and upright; he feared God and shunned evil. He was the greatest man among all the people of the East"* (Job 1:1, 3b). He was a respected elder in his community, admired for his civic leadership and justice.

God granted Satan permission to test Job's righteousness and faithfulness. Within a day Job lost his enormous wealth in livestock, his house, and his servants. Worst of all, his ten children were killed in an accident. Satan *"afflicted Job with painful sores from the soles of his feet to the crown of his head" (Job 2:7).* Job's entire body was wracked with gnawing pain day and night.

As her husband scraped his open sores with pieces of broken pottery, Mrs. Job observed his physical health deteriorating before her eyes. Job struggled with thoughts of shame, insignificance, and injustice. He cried out to God, but heard only silence. Suspecting Job would soon die, and aware of the law stipulating death for blaspheming the name of the Lord (Leviticus 24:16), Mrs. Job suggested a way to hasten her husband's death: *"'Curse God and die'"*

(Job 2:9b). Job refused, saying, *"'Shall we accept good from God, and not trouble?'* In all of this, Job did not sin in what he said" *(v. 10)*. Though stretched to the limits of human endurance, Job refused to give up. He clung to God with all his might.

We expect that the three friends who traveled specifically to comfort Job would have provided encouragement, an oasis in the desert of his suffering. But they offered only a mirage, another disappointment for Job to reconcile. He was subjected to callous arguments from his friends, who branded him a hypocrite. Job craved empathy, dependable counsel, and spiritual guidance, costing his friends nothing, but of significant value to a grieving, afflicted man. Job responded, *"'One should be kind to a fainting friend, but you accuse me without any fear of the Almighty'"* *(Job 6:14, NLT)*.

"The patience of Job" is a platitude that inaccurately describes a major character trait of the Hebrew patriarch. In reality, Job claimed the right to bellow and protest that he was wounded and forgotten by God. Job accused God of excessive criticism (Job 9:23), adamant that he had done nothing wrong to invoke God's discipline or punishment. The more he argued, the more insolence he compiled. Job came perilously close to implicating God of wrongdoing. He deplored what he assumed was God's injustice and insensitivity, accusing God of abusing His power, attacking him, and disregarding his pleas for mercy. *"'You have become cruel toward me. You use your power to persecute me'"* *(Job 30:21, NLT)*. In his fear and loneliness, Job projected anger toward his merciful God.

The believer's spiritual gift of patience includes more than just waiting. It implies calm forbearance of trials without complaining, while relaxing in the comforting arms of Jesus. Serenity and praise are important factors, trusting the plans of God without necessarily knowing His purposes. Patience requires humility and submission to the will of God.

"When we let circumstances come between us and God, God is shut out, and as a result of that we lose the sense of His presence. We get to the place where there is worry and distress instead of peace in our souls, and we do not feel His fatherly hand upon us. We become fretful and impatient and irritable and fault-finding. We get far away from God and out of communication with Him. We do not see the hand of God in all circumstances. All the while He wants to bring us back to Himself in brokenness of heart and humbleness of mind" (J. Vernon McGee).

If we intend to manifest the fine art of patience during adversity, Job is not the model to emulate. Jesus Christ is our divine example. During His thirty-three years on earth, Christ encountered the spectrum of human experiences. Both in His purpose and performance, Jesus patiently carried out the plan established for Him in the heavenly realms. Christ was patient with the Pharisees and Jewish religious leaders whose design it was to taunt and entrap Him. He never sinned. He never lost His temper unjustly. He never dishonored His Father in heaven or people on earth. Jesus was humble and patient with men and submissive to His heavenly Father. The Lord *"is patient with you, not wanting anyone to perish, but everyone to come to repentance" (2 Peter 3:9b).*

Prior to His arrest in the Garden of Gethsemane, Jesus obediently committed Himself to God, praying, "'*Father if you are willing, take this cup {of suffering} from me; yet not my will, but yours be done.'* *And being in anguish, He prayed more earnestly, and his sweat was* *like drops of blood falling to the ground" (Luke 22:42, 44).* Jesus is the perfect, patient Son of God, the only one qualified to atone for mankind's sins.

Though there is no mention of Job's patience in the Old Testament, later Job is commemorated. *"You have heard of Job's persever-* *ance and have seen what the Lord finally brought about. The Lord* *is full of compassion and mercy" (James 5:11).* Job's patience was deficient, but he exhibited steadfast trust and endurance. Job persevered because he had already established a devout personal relationship with God prior to his losses. Though Satan was sure Job would capitulate in defeat under the heavy weight of loss and suffering, he didn't count on his victim's tenacious faith in God. Job's anticipation of his future eternal life in heaven sustained him during the long months of tribulations. *"'At least I can take comfort* *in this: Despite the pain, I have not denied the words of the Holy* *One'" (Job 6:10, NLT).*

We are commanded to *"Rejoice in our confident hope. Be patient* *in trouble, and keep on praying" (Romans 12:12, NLT).* It pleases Jesus to know that His followers inherit His divine attributes. Like anything we learn to do well, we must practice patience, the ability to respond with quiet, uncompromising fortitude under stress. Let us implement the gift of patience that characterizes Christ. Lean hard on the Rock; rest in His divine help and power. Then God will be glorified by our patient, adoring acts of faith.

ATTENTIVE LISTENING

M ary of Bethany, a sibling of Martha and Lazarus, possessed enviable listening skills. When Jesus visited their home, she sat at His feet with rapt attention, hanging on each of her Master's words. Mary unabashedly worshipped Jesus, captivated by her friend to the exclusion of all others present.

On the same occasion, when Mary and Martha prepared a dinner for Jesus and His disciples, Martha demanded. *"'Lord, don't you care that my sister has left me to do the work by myself? Tell her to help me!'" (Luke 10:40).* To Martha's surprise, the Lord commended Mary's actions, tenderly replying, *"'Martha, Martha, you are worried and upset about many things, but only one is needed. Mary has chosen what is better, and it will not be taken away from her'" (vv. 41-42).*

Both Mary and Martha loved their Lord, but Martha allowed distractions to divide her devotion. No doubt her goal was to serve a memorably delicious dinner, employing proper etiquette for her important guests. Martha was ensnared by extraneous details, as so often happens to each of us. It was Mary who displayed compassion, kneeling before Jesus, intently absorbing every word, noticing each gesture, studying His facial expressions, and discerning silent or spoken aspects of His conversation. Mary listened audibly and visually.

On that evening of dinner fellowship six days prior to Christ's crucifixion, Mary poured a pint of expensive perfume over Jesus' feet in anticipation of His upcoming sacrifice. She didn't ask her Lord's permission; she intuitively knew Jesus would approve of her generous, loving act. Surrounded by men, Mary wasn't intimidated. Loosening her long hair to wipe Jesus' feet of excess oil displayed Mary's humility; a respectable woman didn't unbind her hair in public. Her submissive spirit was apparent: caring for feet was servant's work. Mary's actions spoke volumes. By anointing Jesus' feet, she demonstrated that she understood Jesus' role of a servant and His prophesied sacrifice far better than His disciples grasped His teachings.

Listening is an active art, requiring commitment to heed God's directives. To hear well, we must concentrate fully, not permitting diversions to eclipse our attention. Adequate listening skills allow us to know the will of our heavenly Father for our individual lives. We hear God speak to us through His Word as He communicates His love and commands.

The psalmist professed, *"'God has surely listened and has heard my prayer. Praise be to God, who has not rejected my prayer or withheld his love from me!'" (Psalm 66:19-20)*. Prayer time without listening is simply a one-sided conversation, a monologue rather than a dialogue. *"Love the Lord your God, listen to his voice, and hold fast to him. For the Lord is your life" (Deuteronomy 30:20)*.

Prayer and praise, listening and love, complement one another, as we interact with Jesus Christ in a personal relationship.

Centuries ago, God frequently spoke audibly or in dreams to believers. When Jesus ascended to heaven following His sacrificial death and His triumphal resurrection, He sent the Holy Spirit to inhabit believer's hearts. Now the Spirit interprets God's messages and illuminates God's written Word, making His personal guidance and wisdom known to us.

While Jesus was teaching in the temple courts, *"the large crowd listened to him with delight" (Mark 12:37b)*. When was the last time you listened to your Lord during prayer, from His Word, or while reading Christian literature, reacting with extreme interest and great pleasure, the kind of attention Almighty God deserves?

Let us not miss the sovereign plans about which God advises us through His Spirit. Live in anticipation of His message, confident that your two-way communication is functioning to full capacity. More than any other discernable sound in the world, learn to recognize God's soothing words. He provides power to persist toward the ultimate goal of spiritual victory, as we listen, trust, and follow Him.

Prayer reinforces the art of alert listening, as we share our innermost desires with our heavenly Father, who doesn't miss an iota of what we think or say. God is never too distant, preoccupied, or uninterested to harken to the emotions attached to each thought and utterance. Our Lord listens with love. Though He is aware of the intent of our hearts before we speak, God is pleased to hear from us. *"Before they call I will answer; while they are still speaking, I will hear" (Isaiah 65:24).* Of such total concentration and intelligence we have no earthly comparison. God alone is powerful, present everywhere at once, and infinitely knowledgeable.

If we maintain candid, vivacious communication with God, our listening skills will soon produce pleasing acts of worship, as Mary of Bethany demonstrated. Jesus promised, *"'You are my friends if you do what I command'" (John 15:14).* What a privilege, to claim our sovereign Savior as a personal friend, who listens to us and delights in our personal attentiveness to His voice. Could there be any relationship more rewarding?

Before you pray, ask the Holy Spirit to clear your mind of entangled thoughts and diversions, to enable you to focus specifically on God's person and His glory. Then your heart will be receptive to His guidance. In the quietness of your prayer time, ask God to reveal Himself. He will gladly open your mind and heart to disclose paths to follow. *"Listen to my instruction and be wise; do not disregard it. Blessed are those who listen to me" (Proverbs 8:33-34).*

Be attentive to your Savior with the bold singlemindedness Mary exhibited. Incredible interactions occur at the feet of Jesus as we submit, weep, confess, and listen for our Master's divine assurances designed solely for our spiritual victory.

LAMPLIGHTERS

B efore the innovation of electricity, the local lamplighter was a familiar figure. It was his responsibility to illumine city lights at dusk and extinguish them at dawn. Initially, oil or candles were the light sources, later progressing to gas lights. Whatever type of lamp used, the citizens gained a modicum of security during darkness from the predictable illumination of walkways.

Every night at dusk the lamplighter walked or rode between individual lampposts spaced throughout city streets. Some lamplighters carried a ladder, while others gained the appropriate height to reach tall lampposts from the back of a horse. A sole lamplighter extended his staff to ignite each secluded, dark lamp stem with a small flame. Light flooded the space behind the lamplighter as he continued forward to punctuate darkness along his route.

The original source of light penetrating darkness occurred at the creation of the world when God commanded, *"'And, let there be light,' and there was light. God saw that the light was good, and he separated the light from the darkness. God called the light 'day,' and the darkness he called 'night'. And there was evening, and there was morning—the first day" (Genesis 1:3-5).*

Exclusively by His power, God led the Israelites out of captivity in Egypt. He promised His children He would guide them on their journey to the Promised Land. *"You {God} go before them in a pillar of cloud by day and a pillar of fire by night" (Numbers 14:14b).* Just as God's pillars of cloud and fire consistently led the Israelites long ago, Jesus provides His guiding light in our world today. Christ reflects His light to us, and we absorb and disseminate the light of love to others. Jesus said, *"'You are the light of the world. Let your light shine before men that they may see your good deeds and praise your father in heaven'" (Matthew 5:14a,16).* Christ fulfilled His mission as the Light of the World when He walked this earth. Now that He has returned to heaven, Jesus commands believers to continue His light-bearing work.

We are admonished to *"Shine like stars in the universe" (Philippians 2:15b).* When we gaze at millions of stars piercing the night sky with dazzling points of light, we are reminded that God views Christians as His own beacons of light piercing a dark world. It is our purpose to bring glory to God by expanding His outreach of light and good works to others.

In the summertime, twittering fireflies shower the night sky with indeterminable sparkling pinpoints of light. In a similar way, Christians radiate Christ's light in a dark world. If each of us were to introduce one flicker of Jesus' light, individual flashes would be so numerous they would coalesce into a massive glow of love. Kind words, intercessory prayers, or warm smiles convey encouragement, distributing the light of Jesus everywhere.

In the Old Testament, light characterized life and blessings, shining through those who were positive and encouraging. Darkness represented death or evil, often projected in the expression of a grumpy, foreboding person.

By New Testament times, there was no further need of a symbolic representation of God's presence in the pillars of cloud or fire. God's Son, the Light of the World, came to earth to shine glorious love, peace, and grace through His follower's lives. By sacrificially offering His unblemished life to redeem us from sin, Jesus transferred His light to those who love and serve Him.

As Jesus' disciples in current times, believers are the conduit through which God distributes His infinite light in this world. Like a magnet attracts metal, we are drawn to heavenly light. Those who trust in Jesus depend upon Him to illuminate lives and to light walkways. *"Your word is a lamp for my feet, and a light on my path" (Psalm 119:105),* without which we would only grope in darkness.

The old lamplighter left a linear trail of visible light in his path, but we have the ability to perpetuate light in all directions from our lives. We reflect love and joy from Jesus to those whose vision needs the supplemental light of His presence. Immersed in Jesus' light, we are then prepared to minister Christlikeness to others.

Just as the sun supplies the physical light of our world, Jesus embodies spiritual light. *"God is light; in him there is no darkness at all. If we walk in the light, as he is in the light, we have fellowship with one another, and the blood of Jesus, his Son, purifies us from all sin" (1 John 1:5b,7).* The moon has no illumination of its own, reflecting light from the sun. So too, Christians have no inherent light source. Jesus' light is reflected in His followers. We are feckless without a personal infusion from the Light of the World, which enables us access to His profuse energy, irrepressible light, and dynamic power.

Light symbolizes the glory, radiance, and majesty of the Son of God. Light represents the absolute purity and holiness of God, who moves without casting a shadow. His characteristic is light; His light and glory are harmonious. Christ is the lamplighter of our souls. Once His light lavishes our hearts, we are filled to capacity with the inherited qualities of Jesus, spreading the goodness of spiritual light wherever we go. By identifying with Jesus, we appropriate His attributes of love, kindness, and humility.

"For God, who said, 'Let there be light in the darkness,' has made this light shine in our hearts so we could know the glory of God that is seen in the face of Jesus Christ" (2 Corinthians 4:6, NLT). Our spiritual transparency allows the Light of the World to shine through, illuminating the darkness of our surroundings one small light beam at a time. Let us establish heavenly light distribution as a high priority in our outreach to others.

FISHERMAN, FOLLOW ME

S imon Peter's extroverted personality may have been responsible for his leadership role as spokesman for Jesus' select
group of twelve disciples. He was a flamboyant fellow whose
brusqueness created trouble for him and for his Master. Have
you ever pondered the reason Christ recruited Peter as a disciple, when He fully recognized Peter's propensity for aggression?
Though impulsive and roughly hewn on the outside, Jesus looked
into Peter's heart to identify his potential for loyalty, submission,
and reliability. Jesus knew Peter would develop into a powerhouse
for the Kingdom of God in the future. But first, Jesus must sand the
rough edges of Peter's personal approach, teach him tenderness
and tact, and impress upon His disciple the nature of his Master's
mission on earth.

Jesus' disciples were a varied assortment of professions and per-
sonalities. None among them was important or accomplished.
Jesus chose ordinary men to perform extraordinary feats. The most
unprepared were believers He could mold and make into a useable instrument for His glory. Our Lord peers into hearts, searching
for a person's capacity to serve, obey, and to conform to His will.
God's methods have not changed over the centuries. He converts

His weak children to towers of strength to promote His important assignments, as the Spirit infuses them with power and direction.

A life-long fisherman by trade, Peter was self-assertive and independent, intrigued by the authority of the man who urged, *"'Come, follow me', Jesus said, ' and I will send you out to fish for people'"* *(Matthew 4:19)*. Jesus issues the same command to all believers, encouraging us to depend on His leadership for every aspect of our lives. When questions or calamities arise, we need not scramble to find our own solutions. Jesus is our close companion, ready to answer and aid at a moment's notice. In fact, our Savior already knows in advance what will occur in our future. Trusting His guidance offers tranquility when we are surrounded by anxious moments, allowing Jesus to fight our battles and achieve the victories He promises. *"Do not be afraid or discouraged … for the battle is not yours, but God's. Have faith in the Lord your God and you will be upheld"* *(2 Chronicles 20:15, 20b)*.

Peter was impetuous. When he recognized Jesus walking on water, he requested his Master summon him to walk toward Him in the middle of the lake. Peter successfully took several steps on water—until the gusting wind distracted him, and he took his eyes off Jesus. When doubt overwhelmed his faith, he began to sink. *"Immediately Jesus reached out his hand and caught him. 'You of little faith,' he said, 'why did you doubt?'"* *(Matthew 14:31)*. It took courage for Peter to leave the safety of the disciple's boat, depending solely on Jesus to enable him to step onto the surface of the water. In the midst of a storm, whenever our focus is diverted from Jesus, fear claims more prominence than trust. Like Peter, we lose faith and begin to sink from the Master's presence. Jesus is the tangible difference between fear and faith!

The Messiah began preparing His disciples by teaching them about His future suffering and death. *"Peter took him {Jesus} aside and began to rebuke him. 'Never, Lord!' he said, 'This shall never happen to you!' Jesus turned and said to Peter, 'Get behind me, Satan! You are a stumbling block to me; you do not have in mind the concerns of God, but merely human concerns'" (Matthew 16:22-23).* Peter was struggling with unbelief, exposing his own shallow views. Jesus compared Peter's acerbic behavior to that of Satan, as an adversary or an accuser.

At the Passover feast Jesus celebrated with His disciples prior to His crucifixion, Jesus predicted Simon Peter would disown Him three times before the rooster crowed. A few hours later, still vacillating between fear and courage, Peter took his focus off Jesus until the last rooster crowed, the moment when the servant's and the Master's eyes met. *"The Lord turned and looked straight at Peter. Then Peter remembered the word the Lord had spoken to him. And he went outside and wept" (Luke 22:61-62).* How would Peter compensate for such personal failure? By running to the garden, the first of the disciples to greet his risen Savior on Easter Sunday. Later, Peter was the only apostle to be spiritually reinstated by his Lord (John 21:15-17).

Like the audacious disciple, we may be unaware of our own spiritual deficiencies. Following Jesus from afar as Peter did the night of his betrayal, is a dangerous posture for any believer to assume. When we learn to trust Jesus wholeheartedly, there emerges a loyal servant whose sole purpose is to concentrate on the Savior. Let us readily admit the prayer of King Jehoshaphat and his people when they were threatened by enemies: *"'We do not know what to do, but our eyes are on you'"* *(2 Chronicles 20:12),* a prayer that God the Father still honors today.

Simon Peter is a striking example of the transforming power of the Holy Spirit. He was the emboldened orator on Pentecost Sunday three thousand people were converted to Christianity. He had evolved from headstrong to humble, from arrogant to obedient, and from timid to fearless. Peter's spiritual metamorphosis was obvious; he was the first disciple to proclaim Jesus' true identity: *"'You are the Messiah, the Son of the living God'"* *(Matthew 16:16).* Inspired by the Holy Spirit, the uneducated disciple authored two New Testament epistles bearing his name. He was a pillar of the emerging church, and the first apostle to preach the Gospel to the Gentiles. A self-sufficient heart had been rehabilitated into a self-less vessel fashioned for heaven's work!

Due to Peter's transparency, we are confident that each believer's life responds to miraculous spiritual reform. The most bombastic attitude can be tempered and used for God's glory. Our Lord chooses ordinary believers for colossal assignments, strengthening and empowering them with Jesus' attributes. God modified Peter's rebellious characteristics, substituting qualities and sensitivities previously undeveloped in the disciple. All believers are blessed with capabilities that blossom under sovereign tutelage. Jesus is the compassionate Son of God, willing to invest his own perfect life for the purpose of redeeming and reconstructing each of ours.

MUD, FUN, AND WORSHIP

During a summertime pounding rainstorm our toddler teased incessantly to play outside. Finally I relented and clad him in long rubber-coated pants, rain jacket, hood, and boots, wondering if he could possibly move in such restrictive clothing. Never underestimate the will of a toddler! He grabbed his bicycle and rode it the length of our driveway, braking abruptly before reaching his boundary. In the strip of land dividing adjoining house lots, there was a large, shallow mud puddle calling his name. It was at that spot where he parked his bicycle with the training wheels straddling his personal, murky playground.

He hopped onto the bicycle seat, flattened his body into a horse jockey's competitive riding position, and peddled with all the muscle power his little legs could generate. His frantic peddling produced a cascading arc of liquid mud, flinging slime over his body like a spouting geyser. My little boy had been transformed into a chocolate Easter bunny replica, with only his white teeth exposed through a wide, satisfied grin. Immersed in childhood ecstasy, sitting at the center of a mud avalanche, he was enjoying every minute of the onslaught.

It is no surprise that Jesus instructed us to maintain child-like faith in Him. When His disciples assumed that infants and toddlers surrounding Jesus were usurping their Master's limited time, He reminded them of the value of all children: *"'Whoever welcomes one such child in my name welcomes me'" (Matthew 18:5)*. Children naturally know how to laugh and play with unprecedented joy, as they explore the wonders of their surroundings. Verbal squeals reveal their delirious delight with each new discovery. Almighty God, whose glory and authority remains on display throughout heaven and earth, zealously accepts the exalted praise of playful children.

Centuries ago, when a remnant of God's people returned from seventy years of exile in Babylon, their long separation from everything familiar left them with spiritual apathy reflected in disobedience, doubt, and disdain for the worship of their Lord. God assigned His prophet, Malachi, the task of confronting the Israelites with their sins and guiding them into a revitalized, enthusiastically committed relationship with their heavenly Father. *"And you will go free, leaping with joy like calves let out to pasture" (Malachi 4:2, NLT)*. Utilizing a vivid mental picture of frisky, frolicking animals released from the confinement of an enclosed pen, Malachi attempted to invigorate eagerness and passion into his countrymen's lifestyle and worship.

God's Word provides a graphic description of King David vivaciously dancing in a spirit of worship. It was no ordinary occasion. Years earlier, the ark of God, the physical representation of the Lord's presence in Israelite worship, had been confiscated by their Philistine enemies. When King David located the ark, he immediately arranged for it to be reclaimed and transported to the temple. As the ark was ceremoniously carried through the streets of Jerusalem, David could no longer contain his excitement. With grateful animation, *"David was dancing before the Lord with all of his might while he and all Israel were bringing up the ark of the Lord with shouts and the sound of trumpets" (2 Samuel 6:14-15).*

King David jubilantly offered a spontaneous gesture of praise to his sovereign Lord when he performed his solo dance. Because God knows the intent of our hearts, it is apparent He approved of the king's unapologetic ecstasy in celebrating the return of the ark of the covenant, a constant reminder that God resided in their midst, encouraging victorious worship. David's impetuous dance must have resembled the unpenned calves' leap of joy described by Malachi.

David's wife, Michal, criticized what she considered an immoral act, calling her husband's dance vulgar. David responded, *"'In God's presence. I'll dance all I want! Oh yes, I'll dance to God's glory— more recklessly even than this. And as far as I'm concerned... I'll gladly look like a fool... I'll be honored to the end'" (2 Samuel 6:21-22, The Msg.)* Michal was a sourpuss, and like her father, King Saul, she displayed jealousy and bitterness. She manifested the opposite attitude of her husband, King David, who defended his courageous, spontaneous dance to honor the return of the ark of God.

Contrary to the world's view of Christianity as a negative faith consisting primarily of "thou shalt not" regulations, there exists undeniable freedom in following Jesus. Christ himself said, *"'My purpose is to give them a rich and satisfying life'" (John 10:10, NLT).*

It is God's plan that His children live a life of unsurpassed abundance secured by Jesus at Calvary.

"Let the heavens rejoice, let the earth be glad; let the sea resound, and all that is in it. Let the fields be jubilant, and everything in them; let all the trees of the forest sing for joy" (Psalm 96:11-12). Is there any reason we should not join the natural world praising our Creator?

Perhaps a playful mud bath, kicking up your heels, or dancing in a street parade offend your personal preferences. If so, contemplate alternate approaches to glorifying Jesus with heartfelt jubilation. Or follow the example of my friend who surprised me by answering a recent phone call, not with a typical greeting, but by belting out the Hallelujah chorus, an unequivocal reminder for both of us to praise God for an abundant, triumphant life.

Let us join the psalmist expressing exultation for God's rich blessings. *"'I'm thanking you, God, from a full heart, I'm writing the book on your wonders. I'm whistling, laughing, and jumping for joy; I'm singing your song, High God" (Psalm 9:1-2, The Msg.).* Remember King David's unrivaled, but reverent method of praising God whenever you consider adding a new perspective to your personal style of worship.

CARRY ME

I s there any place a child would rather be than hoisted up onto his father's broad shoulders, with legs wrapped securely around his dad's chest, held firmly in his grasp? What a view from the child's perch at the top of his secure world!

The tyke's hands run playfully through his dad's hair until his father suddenly lunges forward, pretending to stumble. Suddenly the child's once-relaxed body contracts in fear. When his quivering hands instinctively reach to grasp something safe, he lands a choke hold on his father's neck. Then his dad laughs uproariously, vowing to play no more tricks. The toddler relaxes again in the shelter of his father's love and protection. The playful ride continues until the duo is happily exhausted.

Being lifted up and revered is not only child's play. Each of us craves protection and the ability to view the world buoyed by the safety of our heavenly Father. *"Let the beloved of the Lord rest secure in him, for he shields him all day long, and the one the Lord loves rests between His shoulders" (Deuteronomy 33:12).*

Our Lord never stumbles nor will He lead us into dangerous territory. When times in our lives are tough, God carries us on His shoulders, the safest place in the world to be. Who among us doesn't long for absolute security and safety? Moses reminded God's people, *"'The Lord your God carried you, as a father carries his son'" (Deuteronomy 1:31).*

Our ride of assurance by God is not a one-time, fun-time. *"'I've been carrying you on my back from the day you were born, and I'll keep on carrying you when you're old. I'll be there, bearing you when you're old and gray; I've done it and will keep on doing it, carrying you on my back, saving you'" (Isaiah 46:3-4, The Msg.).*

When we attempt to navigate inaccessible dreams or the insurmountable trappings of life's circumstances, we are not alone. God, who created us, will sustain us. Relax your tight muscles of fear. Enjoy the promise of your Lord's vast resources of peace and safety; love and kindness; faithfulness and forgiveness.

Just as He led the Israelites into the Promised Land, our Lord also has designed magnificent plans for each of us who faithfully follow Him. God's shoulders are massive, supporting us when we are burdened with a load of care. *"He tends His flock like a shepherd: He gathers the lambs in his arms and carries them close to his heart" (Isaiah 40:11).* Believers are Jesus' lambs; He cares for us as a shepherd.

God delights in His children, lavishing them with love and grace. Let us rejoice in the abundant encouragement God offers. Only then can we enjoy the ride through life held securely on His shoulders, as He hugs us close to His heart.

MARVELOUS MULTI-TASKING

C onsolidating tasks to create efficient use of time is commendable and often successful. Recently I placed a phone call while preparing dinner, an appropriate time saver—or so I thought. As I nestled the phone between my ear and shoulder, both hands were free for other functions. The device soon slipped from its precarious position and launched airborne to clobber an open jar of maraschino cherries. The impact gyrated the jar, spewing cherry juice in puddles on the kitchen countertop, flowing in rivulets down the lower cabinet doors. Before I could predict its next route, sticky liquid accumulated inside my open sandals. My toes were glued in a quagmire of cherry juice. The phone landed keyboard down, in a pool of gooey juice. I was mired in one place, encircled with a smattering of red, syrupy liquid. Cleaning up the cherry debacle took more time than accomplishing each task separately.

Our contemporary lingo is deluged with computer terms, some of which we have adopted for personal use, as with multi-tasking, the concurrent performance of two or more tasks. People have been multi-tasking for centuries; only the name is new. Our Lord is a marvelous multi-tasker who embodies superior knowledge and wisdom, present everywhere at all times. Man may labor to balance a few minor tasks, but our sovereign God accomplishes innumerable enterprises continuously and perfectly every time. He is unlimited in character, actions, and abilities. God never changes, nor is He bound by time or space. God is perfect, divine, and infinite. *"'I the Lord do not change'" (Malachi 3:6).*

God's omnipotence is defined by His superior power and authority. He is capable of answering the prayers of billions of believers while surveilling the entire cosmos. God scans every site of the globe to check on the whereabouts and activities of His children. *"The eyes of the Lord range throughout the earth to strengthen those whose hearts are fully committed to him" (2 Chronicles 16:9).*

As a marvelous multi-tasker, our Lord knits together fractured bones while concurrently painting a breathtaking sunset. His grace miraculously transforms the hearts of believers as He prohibits the worldwide proliferation of communicable diseases. God assigns silk worms to weave elegant fabric while He supervises intricate surgical procedures, imparting knowledge and split second decision-making to surgeons. Our heavenly Father maintains planets in specific orbits, rotating each on an invisible axis at designated speeds as He suspends millions of twinkling stars in space. God presides over the earth, synchronizing balanced ecosystems for the planet and its inhabitants, as He unites people internationally via transportation and communication.

Our Lord monitors the exertional pull of the moon on tidal waters while maintaining exact gravitational forces on the earth's surface. God welcomes one of His dear children into heaven for eternity as He simultaneously greets a newborn baby on earth. He raises

His hand to prevent a vehicular collision while gently unfurling the fragile petals of a rose. All natural elements respond to the Lord's instructions. In one geographic zone, an avalanche of snow plows down a mountainside. On another continent, He paints a perfect rainbow, displaying its prismatic array of colors against a placid, blue sky, reminding us of God's promise to Noah centuries ago.

Our Lord's harmonious efforts impact people and matter everywhere. He is the sole architect and creator of our world, forming it with His commands, sculpting lofty mountain ranges, hollowing vast chasms of earth to flood as oceans, gouging gaping canyons, and leveling large expanses of desert and plains. He travels the labyrinth of galaxies, all the while meeting the complex needs of His children. *"For your ways are in full view of the Lord, and he examines all your paths" (Proverbs 5:21).*

As Jesus followed Jairus, a Jewish synagogue leader, to heal his dying daughter, a crowd impeded their movement. Within the group was a woman who had suffered a bleeding disorder for more than a decade. By tugging Jesus' garment, she gained immediate healing. Jesus interrupted the journey to identify the woman, to announce His miraculous healing, and to commend her faith. Just as Jesus dismissed the woman, a messenger from Jairus' house announced, *"'Your daughter is dead'" (Luke 8:49).* Jesus refuted the report, for He had just performed a multiple healing while delayed by the crowd. When they arrived at Jairus' house, Jesus told the mourners, *"'Stop wailing. She is not dead but asleep'"(v. 52).* Jesus grasped the girl's hand and instructed her to rise from bed, completely cured. Jesus had pronounced Jairus' daughter healed while He was busy with other activities at His previous location, though

He always followed up to interact personally with each afflicted person. There is no limit to our Lord's ability or authority.

God invented marvelous multi-dimensional tasking and He excels in the art, a sovereign version that equips Him with infinite ability to know the end result before the beginning of each endeavor. There is no denying God's knowledge and wisdom. *"O, Lord, you have examined my heart and know everything about me. You know when I sit down or stand up. You know my thoughts even when I'm far away. You see me when I travel and when I rest at home. You know everything I do. You know what I am going to say even before I say it, Lord. You go before me and follow me. You place your hand of blessing on my head. Such knowledge is too wonderful for me, too great for me to understand!" (Psalm 139:1-6, NLT).*

The number of multi-tasks we are capable of juggling at once is of trivial value. Of utmost importance is our relationship to the all-powerful ruler and sustainer of the universe, a personal God who desires to be ever-present in our lives, extending to us righteousness through His Son, Jesus Christ. God possesses superior knowledge and wisdom pertaining to our universe and to each person in it. *"Look up into the heavens. Who created all the stars? He {God} brings them out like an army, one after another, calling each by its name. Because of his great power and incomparable strength, not a single one is missing. Have you never heard? Have you never understood? The Lord is the everlasting God, the Creator of all the earth (Isaiah 40:26; 28a, NLT).* All glory to the majestic skill of the architect and creator of our world!

NEVER CHANGING; ALWAYS NEW

Since the Second World War, the Baby Boomer generation has adapted to an incredible surge of scientific discoveries and technological improvements.

For the first time, airplane travel exceeded the speed of sound, breaking the sound barrier, and disrupting our lives with deafening booms from the sky. Space exploration sent manned flights to the moon with astronauts walking on its surface. Established space stations remain in operation today, accommodating international astronauts who conduct research. Unmanned computer-operated Drones gain intelligence information and at times deploy armaments.

Solar and wind energy, providing clean, efficient alternatives to the use of fossil fuels, are both available for industrial applications and private homes.

Huge strides have been made in the field of medicine in general, but specifically in organ transplant surgery. Most organs are routinely transplanted from a human donor to a recipient, with few cases as dramatic as the replacement heart of an infant.

Cumbersome personal computers were designed, eventually shrunk to laptop or hand-held proportions, and are accessible today by the majority of people. Most corporate and personal data is stored in computers. With a click on the keyboard, numerous tasks are achieved, including retail shopping, studying for a college degree, or paying bills.

Video cameras and cell phones provide the ability to record scenes that can be sent around the world via social media sites. Depending on the amount of interest the subject amasses, it may go viral in a few hours, traveling internationally among subscribers more swiftly than a communicable viral disease. One type of electronic device stores thousands of volumes of books that can be read anywhere by holding a device smaller than a book in one's hand.

Personal vehicles are now routinely equipped with GPS (Global Positioning System), a navigational aid that responds to inquiries for vehicular driving coordinates. A mechanical voice guides the driver until the destination is reached.

Consistently, from the earliest time in the history of the world, God has verbally communicated with His creatures. His promises remain the same today as centuries ago. God not only hears our prayers, but He listens precisely to each word and to the intent of our hearts. *"For the Father knows what you need before you ask him" (Matthew 6:8).* God devised the marvelous method of prayer, permitting us to talk with Him in a two-way conversation, to glorify His name, to intercede for others, or to request our own needs.

Although God maintains foreknowledge of our thoughts, He still desires to communicate with us as a human father lovingly talks with his children. God wants to hear what is interesting and urgent to us, and He longs to direct us toward the paths He chooses for us to follow. More importantly, God desires our praise, gratitude, and glory showered generously upon Him when we pray. What a comfort to know, *"Jesus Christ is the same yesterday and today and forever" (Hebrews 13:8)*

There are no electronic gadgets associated with prayer. Our messages need not bounce among a succession of cell towers before God hears us. Prayer delivery is instantaneous. Jesus, who lives in the heart of every believer, is sensitive to His host, aware of what we intend to say before we speak a word.

There is never interruption of prayer service due to a power outage, or the sudden severance that occurs when an internet provider shuts down for maintenance. Neither does prayer require financial remuneration. There are no limits to the number of minutes we are allowed to talk with God each month. Neither username nor password is required. Our Father easily identifies our voices. He is everywhere present, capable of hearing and answering an unlimited number of prayers simultaneously, and perceptive to our individual needs.

Prayer need never be uttered aloud, nor does another person listen to or receive our messages in error. Prayer is exclusively between us and our Lord, who has power to act immediately on our behalf. God is not merely a receptionist who assigns our requests to angels. We serve a personal Lord, who listens to us individually, delights in each of us (Zephaniah 3:17), supplies all of our needs (Philippians 4:19), and joyfully lavishes believers with love and grace (1 John 3:1).

A computer has no emotions. It is incapable of responding to our most urgent needs. Only God saves and heals, transforming a repentant life to a new one of service, directing us to follow His command to magnanimously love Him and others.

Prayer need not be formal, verbalized, or written. Free your mind to express intimate thoughts and questions to God. Silent prayer is preferred, in which only you and God are involved. Jesus instructed His disciples how to pray: *"'Go into your room, close the door and pray to your Father, who is unseen. Then your Father, who sees what is done in secret, will reward you'"* (Matthew 6:6).

Impatience and fear are inflamed by an instantaneous society, one in which our keyboard fingers, rather than our hearts, control our lives. Take advantage of any opportunity to relax your fast-paced life and silently talk with God, pouring out your heart of love and worship to the awesome, Almighty King of the universe. Despite countless innovative discoveries that will enhance our material lives in the future, nothing will ever surpass the abundance of love, power, and mercy, gifts with which God has lavished mankind since creation.

COMPLACENT

E ach day when traveling to work, I encountered a stretch of res-
idential build-up along secondary roads where the speed limit
decreased twenty miles per hour. Familiar with landmarks along
the route, I typically reduced my vehicular speed in preparation
for the lower speed zone.

One morning a state police vehicle passed me from the opposite
direction. Perceiving I was within the posted speed limit, I ignored
his presence, assuming he had business elsewhere. That is, until
he negotiated a screeching U-turn! Suddenly I was engulfed with
eye-popping blue lights and ear-piercing sirens. The policeman
then had my undivided attention.

When the imposing officer appeared at my car window, he was
straightforward. "Do you know you were traveling 52 m.p.h. in
a 35 m.p.h. zone?" He had the proof; I had no excuse. Still I felt
obliged to offer a weak explanation. "I drive this route to work
every day and I'm usually more compliant with my speed." To
my surprise, the state policeman gently responded, "It's easy
to act complacent when frequently repeating the same activity."
Fortunately the officer dismissed me with a warning. Little did

he know the impression he made that day, not only affecting my driving alertness and compliance, but my approach to other life experiences as well.

Complacency denotes self-satisfaction resulting in false comfort, diminishing an awareness of danger. Apathy and indifference are closely related, expressed by inaction or flat emotions. Passion is the adverse of complacency; zeal the contrast of indifference. Jesus taught that love knows no boundaries, tantamount to the greatest commandment. *"Love the Lord your God with all your passion and prayer and muscle and intelligence—and love your neighbor as well as you do yourself" (Luke 10:27, The Msg.).*

Jesus defined our neighbor by relaying a parable: a man was attacked while traveling from Jerusalem to Jericho through rugged, crime-ridden terrain. He was stripped of his clothing, robbed of his possessions, beaten unmercifully, and left for dead. A Levite, a priest, and a Samaritan eventually passed the victim's way. The first two ignored the assaulted man and intentionally crossed to the opposite side of the road.

Complacency reeks of self-importance. What could possibly have been so pressing in the lives of the Levite and the priest that neither extended the minimal time and compassion to cover the naked, bleeding man with a garment? It is obvious that the suffering victim's pitiful condition didn't tug on their heart strings. For them it was easier to turn away with indifference, while claiming the merit of personal righteousness. Complacency is the greatest hypocrisy.

Historically, Samaritans and Jews exhibited open hostility toward one another. But, it was a Samaritan who ran to the aid of the wretched man lying beside the road. The foreigner bandaged his wounds and lifted him onto his own donkey for transport to a local inn where his benefactor cared for him. The following day, the Samaritan caregiver supplied sufficient funds to the innkeeper, to provide for the injured man's future care, promising to reimburse any extra expenses incurred when he returned (Luke 10:33-35).

The man who posed the question to Jesus, *"'Who is my neighbor?'"* *(Luke 10:29),* learned the answer explicitly from Jesus' parable of the Good Samaritan. Jesus' story defines a neighbor as one we help when a need is apparent, with whom we share our time and treasure, and for whom we are willing to be inconvenienced.

One great danger of complacency is that it gradually conquers the heart space reserved for kindness and decency, bowing to insidious modifications in behavior. Before we are aware of the changes, we've converted to a curmudgeon who increasingly replaces tenderness and passion with ill-tempered responses. What happened to fierce, dynamic faith? It cooled to tepid.

Jesus didn't call us to follow Him when it is convenient. Our time on earth is brief; we are here on assignment. There is kingdom work to be done, people to help, and the Gospel to proclaim. From each of us, Jesus demands the adoration and zeal of total commitment.

What is your response when you recognize a paramount need in another person's life? Do you avoid prayer, assuming Jesus is incapable of surpassing human limitations? *"Jesus replied, 'What is impossible with men is possible with God'" (Luke 18:27).* Continual prayer is our most powerful deterrent to apathy, preventing us from slipping into smug self-dependence and self-satisfaction. Indifference is dispelled by acknowledging that God is supreme and capable of the miraculous. Complacency requires low energy output and no positive returns.

There are blue lights of warning frequently surrounding personal scenarios, reminding us to slow down to discern and evaluate. It is never too late to comply to God's commandment to love others, in which there is no provision for self-serving motives. Complacency and apathy provide only convenient excuses.

The psalmist admitted, *"'You turned my wailing into dancing; you removed my sackcloth and clothed me with joy, that my heart may sing your praises and not be silent. Lord my God, I will praise you forever'" (Psalm 30:11-12).* From the riches of heaven's own wardrobe room, swishing robes of rejoicing distinguish us externally, as Jesus, the source of our praise, engulfs our hearts. Joy is the constant dimension of a life of faith; a sovereign characteristic that flows freely from dwelling in God's presence; a gift that interlocks with God's everlasting nature. Let us reach out to our neighbors with enthusiasm, unafraid to expand beyond our own comfort zones.

Thankfully, neither complacency nor apathy are permanent states, easily remedied with our commitment to spiritual renewal, as we discover the exhilaration of displaying our Lord's characteristics. We are transformed by Christ, a holy reconstruction project uniting us with Him that motivates us to ask, "What can I do to help my neighbor?"

MAGNIFICENCE FROM INSIGNIFICANCE

I n the early history of mankind, God's people followed a predictable pattern of disobedience, prompting God to allow their enemies to conquer and enslave them as punishment for their sins. When the Israelites could tolerate servitude no longer, they cried out to God in repentance. God was merciful and raised up judges to deliver them from oppression and to lead them back into fellowship with Him. Peace was enjoyed for a time until the people once again adopted their neighbor's worship of false gods. Then the cycle revived and revolved as before.

The judges God selected from among the Israelites had no specific knowledge or talent, but God was aware of their potential. *"The Lord does not look at the things man looks at. Man looks at the outward appearances, but the Lord looks at the heart" (1 Samuel 16:7).* The Lord focuses on a person's character and desire to obediently submit to His will.

God calls the lowly rather than the mighty as His helpers. Ehud, the second judge, left-handed and courageous, was qualified for the gruesome task of killing the enemy Moabite king. Because most of his contemporaries were right hand dominant, only Ehud's left side was searched for a weapon before he entered the king's quarters. *"Ehud made a double-edged dagger that was about a foot long, and he strapped it to his right thigh, keeping it hidden under his clothing" (Judges 3:16, NLT).* With his left hand he pulled the dagger from his right side and deftly wielded it to kill the king. Peace ensued in Israel for eighty years.

The nation of Israel had few weapons, but for Shamgar, the third judge, an ox goad was the tool of his trade. A crude instrument used for prodding draft animals, it was a long wooden rod, typically fashioned with a metal tip. The ox goad doubled as a weapon of war that Shamgar used to kill six hundred Philistines, who had been terrorizing the main route of travel used by the Israelites (Judges 3:31). Shamgar learned that no matter how humble, God uses whatever is available for His glory.

When God first called Gideon, he was weak and timid. Before he could serve, God strengthened Gideon's wobbly knees and his cowardly heart, a long, arduous process. God was patient, always upholding the man He chose with His Spirit and power. Weak vessels are the only kind He uses, not wanting men to boast of their own accomplishments, but to glorify God.

Gideon, the sixth judge, was commissioned to save Israel from the Midianites and coalition tribes. As leader of three hundred untrained volunteers, Gideon signaled them to blow trumpets and break empty jars at the precise time appointed by God, scattering the unsuspecting forces. The enemy was pursued and subdued by the Israelites, securing peace in the land for forty years.

After the judges ruled Israel, people begged God for a king, like those who ruled their neighboring countries. Saul, their first king, was initially a donkey wrangler. The people chose Saul based entirely on his physical attributes. Saul was not God's choice, but because the people were insistent, He allowed them to learn a difficult lesson. God was patient and instructive with Saul, permitting him many opportunities to succeed, but Saul didn't give himself wholeheartedly to God or to the people's interests. His monarchy was punctuated with pride, personal ambition, disobedience, and jealousy. David eventually replaced Saul as king. Contrast Saul's performance with that of his successor, God's choice for king. David fervently worshipped God and served the people; King Saul was consumed with his own agenda.

God typically chose people lacking in popularity, riches, or influence to do His work, to lead and to achieve. They had no obvious talents and often possessed glaring faults, sometimes the very reason God chose them. Moses murdered an Egyptian. Jesus' disciple, Matthew, was a despised tax collector. The Apostle Paul initially campaigned to annihilate all Christians. Peter, a disciple, denied knowing his Master on three consecutive occasions. When they followed God, He transformed each person into a personal power house for His kingdom.

God still uses common people for uncommon roles; ordinary folk to perform extraordinary feats. He converts His weak children to towers of strength to promote His important tasks, all of them through the Spirit's power and direction. The weakest and the most unprepared are believers God molds from a previously inadequate person into a useable instrument for His glory. *"Few of you were wise in the world's eyes or powerful or wealthy when God called you. Instead, God chose things the world considers foolish in order to shame those who think they are wise. And he chose things that are powerless to shame those who are powerful. As a result, no one can boast in the presence of God"* (1 Corinthians 1:27, 29, NLT). God's endeavors are supreme and spectacular, identifying His sovereign nature.

If your heart is open to God's love and receptive to His leadership, there is no end to the magnificence He will reveal, as He motivates you to perform at your full potential. You may never be acknowledged as an important person in this world, but God knows your heart is responsive and your goal is obedience. No one who yields to God's molding process remains commonplace. Our Lord only deals in the extravagant and the splendid, lavishing believers with unique abilities to fulfill His missions. *"Each of you has your own gift from God"* (1 Corinthians 7:7). The more we submit to God's will, the greater power with which He equips us.

Believers exercising their own efforts are unable to successfully achieve Christ's objectives. It is only by the power of the Holy Spirit within us, providing strength and enthusiasm, who makes our lives count for Jesus. As obedient children, we are blessed with gifts similar to those of Bezalel, chief craftsman of the sacred ark for God's tabernacle: The Lord *"has filled him with the Spirit of God, with wisdom, with understanding, with knowledge and with all kinds of skills" (Exodus 35:31).* Our personal value is determined by our alliance with Jesus.

Let us offer ourselves unreservedly as instruments for God's purposes. Mortals cannot submit to the immortal without major transformations occurring. Insignificance will always give way to magnificence under God's direction!

FOLLOW OR RETREAT

F lanked by His disciples during His three-year ministry on earth, Jesus traveled incalculable miles by foot and by boat. Wherever they journeyed, curious crowds followed. Some people were sincerely interested in the Messiah's message, but others were simply enamored with His miracles and wanted to see more. News of Jesus' next destination spread quickly; multitudes were often waiting at a future site to meet Him. Though admirers and detractors alike surrounded Jesus, there were two places where throngs tended not to follow. For one, they were disinterested in pursuing Jesus to a secluded spot to pray.

After feeding five thousand listeners by miraculously multiplying one boy's small lunch, Jesus walked up a mountainside to pray alone throughout the evening. Communicating with His heavenly Father, He gained refreshment and renewal of body and soul for the challenging days ahead. Though we are provided no direct insight into the Father and Son dialogue, we know the prominence Jesus assigned to prayer from His detailed instructions to His disciples.

Perhaps the crowds instinctively left Jesus by Himself during His quiet time because, for them, personal prayer was a foreign concept. Temple priests interceded for the people, but few individuals engaged in private prayer. God created and called the nation of Israel; His messages were delivered through prophets. Laws were designated for the entire nation, and the population was often punished collectively for disobedience. There was little communication between individuals and God. By His death and resurrection, Jesus opened the pathway for contact between believers and God the Father, the same intimate fellowship the Son enjoyed.

Calvary was the other area of Jesus' experience people bypassed. Only the Son of God could die a redemptive death on the cross for our sins. Jesus suffered loneliness and agony mankind will never comprehend. It was even necessary for His heavenly Father to forsake His Son for a period as Christ hung on the cross. Only a few of Jesus' close friends and His mother witnessed His crucifixion. All of His disciples but John abandoned their Master, fearing retribution by association.

Prior to His arrest in the garden of Gethsemane, Jesus agonized in prayer. *"He began to be deeply distressed and troubled. 'My soul is overwhelmed with sorrow to the point of death'" (Mark 14:33-34).* Prayer to His Father was His only available source of peace and strength. The soldiers would soon arrive to arrest Him by force. It was not death Jesus feared, but the hour of crucifixion when the weight of the sins of the world—past , present, and future—would transfer to His soul. Jesus bore the unparalleled burden alone.

Crucifixion was a heinous form of death reserved for slaves and the worst Roman criminals. Jesus, the Son of God, the only perfect man to walk this planet, was crucified as a common criminal. Though His enemies intended crucifixion as the ultimate means of persecution to silence Jesus forever, the cross of Calvary became a symbol of Jesus' ability to save mankind, and the believer's commitment to follow only Christ, who willingly sacrificed His holy life for the forgiveness of our sins.

Jesus has redeemed us. Believers now live for Him, infused with His characteristics and identified exclusively with Him. The cross of Calvary is the vehicle that created access to prayer. Jesus' death and resurrection purchased eternity in heaven for every believer. "The cross is a place where one dies to self, enjoys no rights, and grovels in humility. How odd for our Lord to invite us to be crucified with Him; but God knows the cross is a place of grace, and the nearer one draws to Calvary, the more abundant the peace and power" (Joni Eareckson Tada).

Imagine the colossal amount of sovereign power essential for the resurrection and the ascension of our Savior! The same dynamic power is promised to believers. *"I also pray that you will understand the incredible greatness of God's power for us who believe him. This is the same mighty power that raised Christ from the dead and seated him in the place of honor at God's right hand in the heavenly realms" (Ephesians 1:19-20, NLT).*

Jesus' pattern throughout his demanding ministry emphasized solitary time with His heavenly Father. Quality time spent with God provided Jesus with a boost of strength and joy, reinforcing His priorities and purposes on earth. God responded by empowering His Son with love and leadership. If Jesus required frequent replenishing of God's characteristics, how much more often we must request our hearts be invigorated with the benefits God promises. Christ, the perfect Son of God, could not operate independently on earth as a man without perpetual refills of God's attributes. Why, then, do we arrogantly claim self-reliance apart from our heavenly Father? The absolute sufficiency of God reveals the total insufficiency of mankind. *"The earnest prayer of a righteous person has great power and produces wonderful results" (James 5:16b, NLT).*

Let us evaluate our position in prayer and our trek to view the cross, where there is power in the victory the Savior attained for believers. Jesus assures us of blessings aplenty, including life with Him forevermore. If we occasionally withdraw from Jesus, as His disciples were so quick to do at the cross, let us then emulate their future commitment displayed at Pentecost: they prayed for courage to endure, power to carry on their Master's work, and boldness to speak for their Lord. The apostle Paul admitted, *"'I have been crucified with Christ. My ego is no longer central ... Christ lives in me. The life you see me living is not mine, but it is lived by faith in the Son of God, who loved me and gave himself for me'" (Galatians 2:20, The Msg.).*

It is no longer necessary to be jostled by crowds to ensure an audience with Jesus. He is listening this moment, waiting patiently to hear from you. Follow His directions for silent, sincere, steadfast, submissive supplication (Matthew 6:5-8). Jesus encourages us to leave our sins at the cross for forgiveness and to cast our cares at Him in prayer. Let us not retreat from the two important journeys

Jesus traveled on earth, but boldly seek His presence in prayer and in the power of salvation He victoriously secured for us on the cross of Calvary.

KINDNESS IN ACTION

In the orthopedic surgeon's waiting room, several of us were anticipating an X-ray prior to our first post-surgical visit. Seated near me was a man nervously rolling a fistful of medicine bottles in the palms of his hands. He was muttering angrily to his companion in broken English that he couldn't understand the necessity of having another X-ray, and he was "planning to tell them so." Just then, a young, vivacious X-ray technician addressed the distraught man by name and announced, "I'm going to take a quick X-ray before you see the doctor." With great effort he stood up, flashing a sidelong glance at the technician, as if reconsidering his defiant approach.

The technician offered her outstretched arm for him to grasp, asking, "Can I help you?" Even before he replied, she steadied him as they began walking, lightheartedly chatting about the beautiful winter day. It was apparent the man had reformulated his plan of opposition in response to cheerful kindness. If I were to venture a guess about the outcome, I think they had a pleasant visit, with the man's anger dissolving as quickly as the snow melting from his boots.

Although not commonly practiced, the Golden Rule is one of the most universally known commands guiding behavior. The rule instructs us to treat others as we want to be treated. One Bible translation takes our responsibility a step further: *"Here is a simple rule-of-thumb guide for behavior: Ask yourself what you want people to do for you, then grab the initiative and do it for them"* (Matthew 7:12, The Msg.). Since everyone craves compassionate treatment, it is each believer's function to disseminate goodness to others. The vehicle of kindness operates with the fuel of cheer, propelled by good works. Imagine what a pleasant world it would be if each person made kindness a priority.

Some acts of benevolence are premeditated, enacted when we are alerted beforehand to a need. Joshua secretly sent two spies to the walled city of Jericho to assess how best to conquer the land and capture the inhabitants. The king was apprised of the presence of spies in his city, so he confronted Rahab, a prostitute and innkeeper, as to her knowledge of the strangers' whereabouts. She admitted the spies had been to her establishment, but that they had left before the gates of the city were closed at dusk. Rahab deceptively directed the soldiers to follow the spies toward the Jordan River. In reality, she had hidden the two men underneath flax drying on her rooftop.

Rahab informed the secret agents that all of the residents were well aware of the continual miracles their God had performed to rescue and protect the Israelites. She specifically mentioned their knowledge of the parting of the Red Sea. *"'When we heard of it, our hearts melted in fear and everyone's courage failed because of you, for the Lord your God is God in heaven above and on earth below'"*

(Joshua 2:11). In return for the kindness she granted them, Rahab offered to help the spies if they saved her family before the city was destroyed. The men agreed. *"'Our lives for your lives! If you don't tell what we are doing, we will treat you kindly and faithfully when the Lord gives us the land'" (v.14)*. From her window in the city wall, Rahab let the spies down to the ground and instructed them to hide in the hills until the militia abandoned their search in three days.

The mutual kindness between strangers was predicated on trust. For their agreement to succeed, it was necessary for both partners to remain faithful. The spies must remember their promise to Rahab. She agreed to drop a scarlet cord from her outside window to identify the location of her family. Ultimately, all the believers were following the will of God. *"'I am the Lord, who exercises kindness, justice and righteousness on earth, for in these I delight,' declares the Lord" (Jeremiah 9:24b)*. Rahab and her family were saved, she was honored by Joshua, and her name is forever engraved in the lineage of Jesus, the Messiah (Matthew 1:5).

In addition to deliberately planned acts of kindness, we frequently perform random, spontaneous benevolent deeds. We spring into action when a situation presents itself. The moment may not be the most opportune, but in an instant we decide that another's delight or safety is more important than our own convenience. "You cannot do a kindness too soon, for you never know how soon it will be too late" (Ralph Waldo Emerson).

In Jesus' parable of the Good Samaritan, a man was walking from Jerusalem to Jericho, using a route notorious for sheltering opportunistic robbers who ambushed defenseless travelers. The pedestrian was attacked physically, stripped of his clothes and valuables, and left for dead. Both a priest and a Levite passed the beaten, bleeding man, ignoring him by crossing to the opposite side of the road. A Samaritan, hated by Jews and labeled a half-breed, felt pity and came to the aid of the injured man. He anointed the victim with oil and wine and bandaged his wounds. Then he lifted the stranger onto his own donkey, delivered him to an inn, and personally cared for him. The following day the Samaritan gave the innkeeper enough money to house and care for the stranger until he returned, at which time he promised to reimburse any additional costs. (Luke 10:30-37). The parable illustrates the unreserved commitment demanded by the Great Commandment. *"Love the Lord your God with all your heart and with all your soul and with all your strength and with all your mind, and, love your neighbor as yourself" (Luke 10:27).*

On earth, Christ showed kindness to everyone He encountered, regardless of their status. When the Messiah was crucified, His body had already been physically abused beyond recognition. With His last remaining trace of energy, Christ offered compassion to the criminal crucified on the cross beside Him. *"'Truly I tell you, today you will be with me in paradise'" (Luke 23:43).* Christ granted kindness during His worst hour. Surely we can express similar outreach to others during our best of times.

God expects more than civility in our personal relationships; He empowers us to adopt Jesus' attributes. *"As God's chosen people, holy and dearly loved, clothe yourselves with compassion, kindness, humility, gentleness and patience" (Colossians 3:12).* Characteristics that imitate Jesus create a deep stirring of our inner spirits. True character is revealed when the charity that wells up in our hearts converts to tangible acts of lovingkindness toward others.

REVIVE TO THRIVE

"*On the first day of the week we came together to break bread. Paul spoke to the people and, because he intended to leave the next day, kept on talking until midnight. There were many lamps in the upstairs room where we were meeting*" *(Acts 20:7-8)* The Apostle Paul didn't typically preach a marathon sermon, but the believers in Troas hungered to feast their souls on the Word of God, creating a sweet spirit of fellowship during the last night of Paul's week-long visit.

Many torches provided the light source in the upstairs meeting room, probably creating a poorly ventilated, unusually warm environment. A young man named Eutychus was sitting in an open window. By midnight, as his eyelids grew heavy and his body relaxed, he fell sound asleep, abruptly toppling out the window, dying instantly when he hit the ground three floors below. *"Paul went down, threw himself on the young man and put his arms around him. 'Don't be alarmed,' he said, 'He's alive.'" (Acts 20:10).*

Before ascending to heaven, Jesus empowered His apostles with sovereign authority. *"'Heal the sick, raise the dead, cleanse those who have leprosy, drive out demons'" (Matthew 10:8).* The Son of

God sent His apostles to minister with credentials similar to what He possessed. The risen Christ enabled Paul to revive Eutychus from premature death with specially endowed powers. *"The people took the young man home alive and were greatly comforted" (Acts 20:12).*

Historians attest that Jesus healed thousands of suffering people during the span of his three-year ministry on earth, though we have anecdotal records of only a small cross-section of complete cures. *"Jesus performed many other signs in the presence of his disciples, which are not recorded in this book. But these are written that you may believe that Jesus is the Messiah, the Son of God, and that by believing you may have life in his name" (John 20:30-31).*

Each healing miracle by Jesus was magnificent and unique. To individualize health restoration, Jesus rarely employed the same technique twice. He made a mud pack, applied it to one man's eyes, and restored his sight (John 9:6). Jesus' ability was endless, as He demonstrated by converting the dust of the earth into a medium of healing. Another time people brought to Jesus a deaf mute for healing. *"He put his fingers into the man's ears. Then, spitting on his own fingers, he touched the man's tongue. Looking up to heaven, he sighed and said, 'Ephphatha,' which means, 'Be opened!'" (Mark 7:33-34, NLT).* Instantaneously, the man could speak and hear perfectly without instruction or coaching.

Ministering with an overwhelming pattern of wellness on earth, Christ faithfully fulfilled Old Testament prophecy from centuries earlier: *"Then will the eyes of the blind be opened and the ears of the deaf unstopped. Then will the lame leap like a deer, and the mute tongue shout for joy" (Isaiah 35:5-6).*

Jesus' most frequently repeated act of compassionate healing involved His personal touch, conveying gentleness and lovingkindness as He laid His hands on the affected body part. Imagine the impact His gesture of touch made on the leper, who had received no personal contact for years. According to Jewish law, those suffering with leprosy were required to live in colonies outside of town, an early form of quarantine. *"A man with leprosy came and knelt in front of Jesus, begging to be healed ... Moved with compassion, Jesus reached out and touched him ... He said, 'be healed!' Instantly the leprosy disappeared, and the man was healed" (Mark 1:40-42, NLT).*

Once Jesus ascended to heaven, He delegated healing authority to His apostles on earth. Neither Jesus nor His methods have changed. Our modern healthcare workers perform sophisticated medical treatments, surgery, and transplants only because the Great Physician provides knowledge and wisdom to man, combined with His own miraculous healing.

On earth Jesus could have cured every disease with one stroke of His sovereign hand. But Jesus always reinstated health for the benefit of spirit and body. Complete cleansing was His goal. He confirmed that the person He cured believed in Him, requiring that Jesus interact with each individual.

God's plans are perfect. He knows the outcome before we are aware of a problem. Though believers aren't always informed of

His purposes regarding their future health status, He consistently promises more of Himself: His love, presence, and comfort for our spiritual wellness. God *never* abandons us to our own unreliable resources. And, He is fully capable of confounding earthly physicians with miraculous healings they cannot explain in scientific terms.

God designs our immune systems with the innate ability to release microscopic armies of militia cells to combat toxins that invade during illness. He strengthens our mental tenacity and physical endurance to wait upon Him for improvement or cure. God created you; He knew you before you were born, and continues to care for you throughout your entire lifetime. God delights in you and loves you in enormous proportions.

Aren't you thrilled that God is the Master Physician responsible for your medical care? He has more education, more experience, more patients, and the best healing rate on the planet. You will never wait for an appointment; His services are complementary. His power and authority extend throughout heaven and earth. And, His Son practices with Him to provide the most superlative healthcare available. Father and Son answer every call personally. Where could you locate another physician so divinely invested in your life?

On the cross, our Savior suffered the very depths of human depravity to restore the sinner's spiritual wellness. Trust the Savior, the Great Physician, for He is always available and responsive to you.

ROSE OF SHARON

C ultivated extensively for the past five thousand years in the Middle East, rose petals were used for confetti in ancient celebrations, for medicinal purposes, and as a source of perfume. Seventeenth century royalty used both rose blossoms and rose water as payment or for barter. Designated as a tangible expression of love in our current age, what conveys affection or adoration more obviously than a bouquet of roses? Though long ago a cherished flower of nobility, roses of all varieties are now commonly grown by novice gardeners.

Roses are designed and proliferated throughout the land by our Lord, the Master Creator. There are no color clashes in God's world; pink, red, orange, purple, fuchsia, and yellow exist in an array of hues, blooming side-by-side in natural harmony, illustrating the cooperative manner in which our Creator intends for people of all nationalities and ethnicities to function. The Lord Jesus claimed, *"'I am the rose of Sharon, a lily of the valleys'" (Song of Songs 2:1)*, in whom the preeminence of God is revealed.

"For God, who said, 'Let light shine out of darkness,' made his light shine in our hearts to give us the light of knowledge of God's glory

displayed in the face of Christ" (2 Corinthians 4:6). Jesus came to earth from the presence of God in heaven, the perfect Son, lovely to gaze upon, to exalt, and to emulate. He lavishes pleasure through our senses, intensifies our praise, and magnifies our worship of the Godhead. Jesus is splendid and majestic! When He identifies with the rose of Sharon, He is portrayed as a beautiful, stately blossom thriving in the fertile valley of Sharon in Palestine, where the elegant flower grew in profusion.

Jesus, the personified Rose of Sharon, radiates love, fragrance, and delight. He captivates our minds as we seek Him, dwells in our hearts as we absorb His love, and permeates our speech as we exhale ministering words of devotion to him. *"Taste and see that the Lord is good" (Psalm 34:8a).* Both the Father and the Son engage our senses, that we may fully experience their glowing splendor. We are reflectors of sovereign light, bearing the image and beauty of God as we derive our very life from Him. Similar to the way a delicate bud opens from the center to reveal glamorous layers of rose petals; our hearts display the nuclei of our spiritual lives where Jesus' love multiplies.

Physical attraction is rarely emphasized by our Lord, though man's priorities are often determined by personal beauty. God is far more interested in the integrity of man's inner character, *"the unfading beauty of a gentle and quiet spirit, which is of great worth in God's sight" (1 Peter 3:4).* Hearts predisposed to seeking purity arouse reverence toward God.

Let us behold Christ's righteousness and holiness as He occupies our thoughts and affirms our priorities. In a world infiltrated with thorns of danger, the Rose of Sharon is poised to deluge believers with comfort and compassion.

Witnessing the unfolding of God's glory in the Son must have been an ecstatic experience for those who glimpsed His presence on earth. It is no small wonder that masses were attracted to the blessed one of God. His purity was breathtaking, set apart from all humanity. We still marvel with delight at Jesus' glory and righteousness.

The believer responds to Christ on a spiritual level. Hearts are transformed by the Savior's love and saving grace. Like the predictable maturing of a rose from bud to blossom, the believer's faith unfolds with beauty, gentleness, and joy, one petal of obedience at a time. Blossoming love is accomplished by Christ's residence in the believer's heart.

Roses need abundant sunlight to bloom, just as Christians crave the abiding presence of Jesus' splendor and majesty to flourish. As we diligently remain united with Christ through faith, we reflect His beauty in our lives. *"As God's chosen people, holy and dearly loved, clothe yourselves with compassion, kindness, humility, gentleness and patience" (Colossians 3:12),* features of our inner selves highly valued by God.

A rosebud is encased in a snug package, gently swaddled by a few guardian outer leaves. As the flower matures, the leaves relax, permitting each subsequent layer to expand to full capacity. Our hearts jubilantly respond like a newly exposed rose blossom, revealing a delightful uniqueness, radiantly shining with the light of Jesus, and stunning the world with the intense fragrance of Jesus' divine love. Just as the flower bud's true potential is revealed when its exterior sheath peels away to unveil a shining rose within, Christ living in each heart promises a unique positional status as a child of the King and heir with the Son of God for all eternity.

In every one of His marvelous designs, our Creator is visible. Ponder the unique shapes and intricate details God invests in individual roses. He is not reluctant to spend extravagant artistry on each flower, utilizing variegated colors and velvety softness to enhance a blossom. Then God lavishes specific plants with His proprietary fragrance, poured with impunity from His heavenly lab into gardens on earth.

"Christ loved us and gave himself up for us as a fragrant offering and sacrifice to God" (Ephesians 5:2). As a renowned rose, Jesus is the object of extreme beauty and humility. Voluntarily leaving His majestic throne and exalted oneness with His Father in heaven, Jesus descended to earth as the Son of man, espousing meekness and gentleness. Living anywhere below the glory of heaven necessitated that Jesus embrace humility to characterize His earthly ministry.

Christians exude the beauty of Jesus in unrivaled form and fragrance. A joyful attitude, a forgiving spirit, and acts of kindness place followers of Christ in unparalleled positions to bountifully disseminate the soothing aroma and character of the Rose of Sharon.

BLEATING OF THE SHEEP

H istorically God's chosen people displayed chronic patterns of disobedience. Nearly as soon as God communicated new decrees, the Israelites either ignored or blatantly disobeyed them. Few people took God seriously; fewer still took His commands seriously. In Old Testament times, the punishment for breaking God's laws was particularly severe: disease, pestilence, capture by enemy forces, and sometimes immediate death. Yet the extreme consequences were insufficient to motivate the Israelites to consistently obey their Lord.

The prophet, Samuel, relayed God's instructions to King Saul: "'Now go, attack the Amalekites and totally destroy all that belongs to them. Do not spare them; put to death men and women, children and infants, cattle and sheep, camels and donkeys'" (1 Samuel 15:3). The Amalekites were descendants of Esau, named after his grandson, Amalek. The directions were simple in terms of clarity. King Saul understood explicitly.

His directive may seem excessively harsh, but God and the Israelites knew the Amalekite people to be sinister and savage. They were predatory, attacking the Israelites during their wilderness walk.

From the rear of the camp, the Amalekites stalked and killed the weak and the elderly as they traveled from Egypt. Their treatment of Israel was spontaneous and vicious, causing Moses centuries earlier to prophesy: *"'When you were weary and worn out, they {Amalekites} met you on your journey and attacked all who were lagging behind; they had no fear of God. When the Lord your God gives you a rest from all the enemies around you in the land he is giving you to possess as an inheritance, you shall blot out the name of Amalek from under heaven. Do not forget!'" (Deuteronomy 25:18-19).*

God had been generously patient with the Amalekites, allowing them over five hundred years to change their barbaric ways. Our heavenly Father is the supreme judge, adjudicating wrong and evil. He does not forget!

King Saul was provided the opportunity to demonstrate his faithfulness to the Lord by obeying his assignment to annihilate the Amalekite nation. With thousands of soldiers He staged an ambush, but instead of wiping out all life, *"Saul and the army spared Agag {the Amalekite king}, and the best of the sheep and cattle, the fat calves and lambs—everything that was good. These they were unwilling to destroy completely but everything that was despised and weak they totally destroyed" (1 Samuel 15:9).*

God then spoke to the prophet, Samuel, expressing sorrow that He had ever anointed Saul king of His people, for Saul refused to follow God's instructions, relying on his own instincts and greed instead. When the prophet, Samuel, confronted King Saul, he discovered the king had established a monument in his own honor.

From disobedience to false image worshipping, King Saul was puffed up with self-importance. Yet even before Samuel questioned him, Saul offered, *"'I have carried out the Lord's instructions'" (1 Samuel 15:13)*. King Saul actually believed his actions were appropriate, but sinning against God is neither wise nor justified. The prophet retorted, *"'What then is this bleating of the sheep in my ears? What is this lowing of the cattle, that I hear?'"* *(v.14)*. King Saul shifted responsibility, blaming the soldiers for sparing the best animals to use as temple sacrifices for the Lord. Samuel then shrieked, *"'Enough!'"* (v.16).

Envision the prophet abruptly gesturing with his hand, protesting King Saul's weak excuses. The prophet asked King Saul, *"'Why did you not obey the Lord? Why did you pounce on the plunder and do evil in the eyes of the Lord?'"* *(v. 19)*. It appears the details of God's commands were irrelevant as long as Saul met his own selfish desires. Later King David explained correct heart health: *"'My sacrifice, O God, is a broken spirit; a broken and contrite heart'"* *(Psalm 51:17)*. Our Lord values humility, repentance, and grief for sin. King Saul's heart was infested with pride and greed. God removed His Spirit from Saul, dethroned him as king of Israel, and anointed another king in his place.

During self-examination, have we made the awkward discovery that we are as shrewd as Saul, crafting insidious excuses for disobeying God? What personal justification do we use when God confronts us with our sins? We have ready access to God's Word through which He speaks to us. God commands that we love Him and others more highly than ourselves, discouraging selfish motives.

It is possible that fear of reproach prevents us from sinning on a regular basis, but we occasionally fall into temptation that is hard to resist. That is when our obedient devotion and love of God is paramount to empower us to follow His words and His will. *"He has shown you, O mortal, what is good. And what does the Lord require of you? To act justly and to love mercy and to walk humbly with your God" (Micah 6:8).* It is a condensed, compelling principle of behavior, defining a right relationship of believers with Almighty God.

Our Lord loves us immeasurably, demonstrated by the gift of His Son, who died to set us free, creating a spiritual bridge between finite humans and the infinite heavenly Father. With God's overwhelming love and attention to every detail in our lives, why would we even consider disobeying Him, with the intention in self-satisfaction? *"Anyone who claims to be intimate with God ought to live the same kind of life Jesus lived" (1 John 2:6, The Msg.).*

We cannot come to God without faith in Him; faith leads to obedience. We want to please our Savior by serving Him. It grieves our Lord when we wander outside the boundaries He has established for us. *"'You are my friends if you do what I command. I have called you friends, for everything that I learned from my Father I have made known to you'" (John 15:14, 15b).* It is astounding that human friendship with Jesus is at all possible, deeming it imperative that we not react to His gracious gift with apathy or scorn associated with disobedience.

Instead of responding like King Saul, blaming others for rebellion against God's authority, Our Lord expects us to take personal responsibility for sin, redirecting our focus to serve Jesus as friends and fellow workers, seeking to consistently pursue His righteousness and faithfulness. Obedience to God is palpable evidence of our faith. God considers our personal submission to His will so expressive of our love for Him that He accepts full responsibility for the consequence of our obedience.

PERFECTION AND DECEPTION

G od placed Adam and Eve in the luxurious garden He planted in the Fertile Crescent of the Middle East. The Garden of Eden was self-supporting. Fruit-bearing trees were abundant, four rivers ran through it, and plentiful plants yielded nourishing food. Rain never fell; irrigation occurred by gentle mists rising from the ground. No pests invaded green plants; everything was pristine and pure. Such incomparable beauty and flourishing opulence would overwhelm us with its splendor, but to the first inhabitants, it was simply home, the only residence they had ever known.

The two people who walked in the exquisite environment of the garden, who bathed in the clear, cool rivers, and who communicated constantly with their Creator, enjoyed freedom and abundance in the fertile, life-sustaining garden. There were no flaws in their lives or surroundings. They were created in an untarnished, sin-free world.

"Now, the serpent *was more crafty than any of the wild animals the Lord God had made" (Genesis 3:1).* Satan questioned Eve about God's authority and the accuracy of His specific directions regarding the one tree from which they were instructed not to eat.

Satan baited Eve, tempting her to gaze at the tree of knowledge of good and evil. The fruit may have suddenly acquired a tantalizing appeal to Eve. Neither person had previously been exposed to the forbidden tree. If any of us devote time where we do not belong, view or read that which is harmful, we too, begin to see beauty or advantage in the detrimental. We often defend our thoughts and actions by the world's standard: the end justifies the means. God's principles are measured by distinct criteria: *"Test everything. Hold onto the good. Avoid every kind of evil" (1 Thessalonians 5:22).*

Though temptations constantly swirl about, God commands us to watch and pray, to demonstrate discernment, and to uphold Jesus as our model. *"Be imitators of God, therefore, as dearly loved children" (Ephesians 5:1).* For a moment Adam and Eve were overcome with opportunity and greed. Disobedience banished them from the garden forever. Instead of death, as God had initially warned, they were evicted from their perfect, palatial garden home and assigned to a foreign, fallen world, to toil hardscrabble land forever.

During His forty-day temptation in the wilderness, the devil offered Christ the opportunity to circumvent His original purpose on earth in exchange for food, material riches, and power (Matthew 4:1-11). Satan's ultimate goal was to convince Jesus to bow down to worship him instead of His heavenly Father, tempting Him to bypass death on the cross as His sacrifice for mankind's sins. Jesus is sinless, with characteristics of purity and holiness that couldn't possibly yield to Satan's wily ways, or He would compromise His sovereign character. Jesus quoted Old Testament scripture as a retort to each of Satan's enticements.

It was imperative for Christ to experience temptation as a man, claiming God's power to send Satan slinking away in utter defeat. Jesus was tested to prove His sinless nature as our Savior, on whom we can depend when we are seduced by Satan and his cohorts. Jesus' trials covered the entire spectrum of human temptations. He personally experienced the devastating damage wielded by Satan's demonic powers, validating that human effort is inadequate; God's power is invincible.

Christ was successful in rejecting the temptation of the devil by immersing Himself in prayer. His example promotes intimacy with God. When we are enticed by temptations, we are commanded: *"Submit yourselves, then, to God. Resist the devil, and he will flee from you. Come near to God and He will come near to you" (James 4:7-8).* Our Savior acts as our barrier for the destructive influence of Satan. Jesus is the pure, holy Son of God, who teaches us by example that men live *"on every word that comes from the mouth of God" (Deuteronomy 8:3b).*

Believers are privileged that God desires to communicate and fellowship with them. The Word of God and prayer are powerful deterrents for evil. *"Ask God to give you complete knowledge of his will and to give you spiritual wisdom and understanding. Then the way you live will always honor and please the Lord" (Colossians 1:9-10, NLT).* Continual prayer prepares us with strength to resist temptation, knowledge to avoid Satan's charm, and wisdom to claim God's power as our own.

Satan, the professional tempter, is a connoisseur of confusion and chaos. As Christians, our emphasis is shining Christ's light into darkness to reveal Satan at his schemes. *"For he {God} has rescued us from the dominion of darkness and brought us into the kingdom of the Son he loves, in whom we have redemption, the forgiveness of sins" (Colossians 1:13-14).* As we saturate our lives with prayer, we are empowered, and the Son of God is glorified.

On the Mount of Olives, where Jesus prayed alone prior to His arrest, He commanded His sleepy disciples to remain on guard against evil forces. *"'Watch and pray so that you will not fall into temptation. The spirit is willing, but the body is weak'" (Matthew 26:41).* On earth, Jesus was perpetually tempted, just as we are. Now as our advocate in heaven, He pleads to the Father for our benefit, fully aware of the natural tenacity and supernatural power required to diligently resist temptation.

Christians are engaged in spiritual battles fighting Satan and his demons, but God has not left us defenseless. Our most dangerous enemies in this world are invisible, not to be fought with brute force, but with the unique spiritual equipment God furnishes: truth, faith, peace, righteousness, salvation, and the Word of God (Ephesians 6:14-17). Jesus, who defeated Satan on the cross, also provides prayer, our greatest military arsenal for life's battles.

Though our trials are often intense, we are endowed with the spiritual weapons God designed. Be prepared through prayer and knowledge of Scripture, to deflect Satan's fiery arrows with determined conflict, just as Jesus demonstrated. "Satan tests us at our weakness, so that he might destroy us; but God tests us at our strengths, so that He might employ us" (Dr. David Jeremiah).

CRUSHED BUT NOT BROKEN

C rowds of people pose unique and bizarre dynamics. Peaceful assemblies meet to discuss, to learn, or to resolve issues. The dedicated enthusiasm of sports fans in a stadium or retail shoppers at a sale may degenerate into frenzied pushing and shoving, heightened by difficulty of individual movement when a group is compacted into a small space. Some folks may be physically propelled by the energy or direction of a multitude. Overzealous behavior at rallies may lead to injury and violence. Complaining or demonstrating throngs of people may transform into a mob. Anyone attempting to exit a gathering could be trapped from within and seriously harmed. Efforts to manage large crowds of people are frustrating, the results often as catastrophic as stampeding animals.

Jesus was frequently the victim of crowd manipulation. *"As Jesus was on his way, the crowds almost crushed him" (Luke 8:42b).* Some of those gathered around Jesus were thirsty for knowledge or in need of healing; others yearned to witness Jesus' miracles. Located in the midst of the crowd where He was pushed and jostled, Jesus retained the compassion to focus on one person, patiently discerning individual needs and providing the specific attention required.

When Jesus detected a tug on His robe, He recognized power had left Him. He demanded, *"'Who touched me?' When they all denied it, Peter said, 'Master, the people are crowding and pressing against you'" (Luke 8:45).* Peter informed his Master of the futility of locating the individual within a large, fluctuating number of curious followers. Not satisfied with Peter's complacent attitude, Jesus persisted. He identified the person's touch as light but deliberate. Someone had a motive of healing in mind! The moment the woman with the twelve-year history of a hemorrhagic disease touched Jesus' robe, her bleeding immediately ceased (v. 47).

At the time of the woman's healing, Jesus was on His way to heal another person, but suddenly He stopped, diverting His attention to the person in the crowd who transferred healing power from His body by tugging His garment. Jesus wouldn't permit the woman to slink away without commending her faith and assuring her of the permanence of her healing. That memorable day she learned, *"The Lord searches every heart and understands every motive behind the thoughts. If you seek him, he will be found by you" (1 Chronicles 28:9).*

Jesus' reaction to a gentle outreach on His clothing or on His heart always activates a tender, compassionate response. What prevents us from calling on Him for each one of our needs, whether minor or major? *"Then you will call, and the Lord will answer; you will cry for help, and he will say: 'Here am I'" (Isaiah 58:9).*

Every day we are bombarded with challenges to our faith. Calamities occur that threaten our ability to function: financial devastation, serious health issues, frayed relationships, loss of employment. We feel crushed by the enormity of the situation. We doubt recovery. We grieve losses. We are discouraged and distressed. Where do we find solace?

On earth, Jesus routinely escaped His followers, favoring a place of solitude and prayer. He sought spiritual enrichment from His Father to fill His heart with heavenly goals and His mind with sovereign wisdom. By continually seeking God's will, Jesus renewed His strength and clarity of mission. We aren't aware of the specific content of Jesus' prayers, but we have evidence of the result: refreshment, renewal, rejoicing. For the Son of God, it was an opportunity to evaluate His priorities and to problem-solve; to worship and to glorify the Father. Jesus' preference of seclusion in prayer is the example He instructs believers to follow.

Our Savior understands reactions of disappointment, discouragement, and disillusionment, for He experienced similar emotions as an incarnated man on earth. Jesus was the subject of disbelief by His own siblings. He was humiliated, disrespected, criticized, and falsely attacked by opponents. Church leaders detested Him and sought His annihilation. What was His response? *"Very early in the morning, while it was still dark, Jesus got up, left the house and went off to a solitary place, where he prayed" (Mark 1:35).* Jesus spent quality time in secluded, secret prayer with His heavenly Father, providing Him with the high energy levels necessary to accomplish God's will for His challenging ministry.

God's children aren't exempt from troubles, but God assures us that He will comfort, protect, and strengthen those who cry out to Him for deliverance. Our Lord is faithful, the unfailing liberator of the righteous. When Jesus was crushed by crowds, the masses were unable to adversely affect His ability to minister to individuals within the throngs. Jesus hasn't changed. He still listens intently to our prayers and intercedes with victory for believers. *"The Lord is close to the broken hearted and saves those who are crushed in spirit. The righteous person may have many troubles, but the Lord delivers him from them all" (Psalm 34:18-19).* How can we possibly resist such pure love and compassion?

Call on Jesus, lavishing Him with praise and gratitude. Call on Him to communicate and maintain a consistent bond of fellowship. Jesus wants to supply you with joy of heart and peace of mind. Assured that our heavenly Father is within easy access invites us to confide in Him anytime, anywhere. *"How gracious he {God} will be when you cry for help! As soon as he hears, he will answer you" (Isaiah 30:19b).*

We may be crowded by energetic groups of people, as Jesus was, or we could be crushed by circumstances beyond our control. Jesus possesses the desire and the ability to rescue us from adversity. We are commanded to worship our Lord in the splendor of His majesty, glorifying His name at every opportunity. Father and Son deserve our personal best, for they have sacrificed their ultimate for each of us!

THANKSGIVING FOR
THE THANKWORTHY

I n 1621, the first Thanksgiving in America was a mutual endeavor between culturally diverse Native Americans and newly arrived colonists for a feast to celebrate the pilgrims' first harvest in the New World. Since the 1800s, annual Thanksgiving feasts have been observed in America. Congress passed a joint resolution establishing a permanent, annual day of Thanksgiving, designated as the fourth Thursday in November, to commence in 1942. The legal holiday was founded as a religious observance for all citizens to express thanksgiving to God for His blessings during the previous year.

In centuries past, the Israelites observed mandatory thank offerings and specific feasts several times each year, a periodic reminder for worshippers to lavish their heavenly Father with praise for abundant harvests and consistent blessings.

It is common to minimize a thank-you as simply a demonstration of good manners. For Christians, thanksgiving exceeds etiquette and yearly feasts. Believers embrace a perpetually grateful attitude, a pattern as natural as breathing, emerging from a heart in tune with the heavenly Father. A life permeated with gratitude effervesces like water surging headlong over a steep precipice, producing prisms of scintillating rainbows in sunshine.

During their escape from centuries of slave labor in Egypt, millions of Israelites traveling on foot stopped abruptly when confronted with the hopeless task of crossing the Red Sea. *"Nothing is impossible with God" (Luke 1:37).* He rolled the water upward, exposing a path of dry land for the people to walk through the sea. As soon as the last remnant of God's people safely reached the opposite shore, the pursuing Egyptian army and weapons were swallowed by the returning walls of water. In response to the Lord's spectacular deliverance of His people, the entire Israelite nation praised God with songs of gratitude for His power, authority, and majesty (Exodus 15:1-21).

Hannah and Elkanah were married, but childless, in a culture where barren women were often harassed until their spirits were crushed with shame and reproach. At the tabernacle, Hannah poured out her heartbreak to God in a passionate prayer, pleading for a son. Sometime later Hannah gave birth to a boy. As she had promised God in her prayer, Hannah delivered Samuel to the priest for a lifetime of dedicated service at the temple (1 Samuel 2:1-10).

Hannah's song of gratitude proclaims that life and death, wealth and poverty, humility and triumph are all determined by a personal, powerful God. Hannah professed that God functions in exalted ways we neither predict nor fully understand, but He always answers believers' prayers in unexpected, extraordinary ways. Hannah's joy was unsurpassed for the gift of a son for whom she expressed supreme gratitude to God for His lovingkindness. She worshipped the Almighty as the exclusive source of sovereignty, unique and powerful throughout the ages.

The Magnificat (Luke 1:46-55), is one of the most familiar songs of thanksgiving in Scripture, composed by Mary following the angel's announcement that she had been chosen as mother of the promised Messiah. Mary glorified God, affirming His mercy, might, and magnificence; His unfailing love and goodness. As words of praise spilled from her grateful heart, Mary acknowledged God had chosen His humble servant for an exalted assignment.

Adoration praises God for who He is. *"Call to the Lord who is worthy of praise" (Psalm 18:3).* Thanksgiving expresses gratitude for what God has done. Believers pray with confidence, assured our Lord will answer each petition. Since we attest to God's faithfulness, anticipating responses to our prayers yields a spirit of thanksgiving, assured God's replies will always reflect His perfect will. Trust, then, is a form of worship whereby we thank God in advance for his blessings. *"Don't worry about anything; instead, pray about everything. Tell God what you need, and thank him for all he has done. Then you will experience God's peace, which exceeds anything we can understand. His peace will guard your hearts and minds as you live in Christ Jesus" (Philippians 4:6-7, NLT).* Prayers of His people invite God's extravagant blessings.

God's plan of salvation and Jesus' willingness to sacrifice His holy life for the redemption of our sins evoke prayers of thanksgiving. Praise is our method of offering heartfelt joy to the Father and Son. *"But thanks be to God! He gives us the victory through our*

Lord Jesus Christ" (1 Corinthians 15:57). It is important to recognize the myriad blessings our Lord bestows on us every day: wellness of body and mind, restful sleep, plentiful water and food, reliable transportation, secure homes, family, and employment. Gratitude naturally pours from a believer's humble, joy-filled heart.

"Give thanks in all circumstances; for this is God's will for you in Christ Jesus" (1 Thessalonians 5:18). The word, "all" is tiny but inclusive, enveloping the whole of one's time, treasure, talent, triumph, and tragedy. God desires our consistent gratitude through the good and the bad, in delightful and challenging situations, all for the purpose of maturing our faith and offering Him glory and honor. *"Through Jesus, therefore, let us continually offer to God a sacrifice of praise—the fruit of lips that openly profess his name" (Hebrews 13:15)*. Thanksgiving is the springboard to spiritual joy.

Worship consists of praise, adoration, song, and prayer, aspects of thanksgiving that convey love and reverence to the sovereign Father and Son. The contemporary use of worship is derived from the old English word, "worthship," denoting the worthiness of God. Thankworthy reflects gratitude through worship. No one exemplifies worship of the heavenly Father more perfectly than Jesus, who offered the ultimate sacrifice of praise, the motivation for a life overflowing with thanksgiving. Jesus is the standard of worship to the Father, a heavenly portrait of goodness and grace. The very essence of thanksgiving compels King David's jubilation. *"'Thank you! Everything in me says thank you! Angels listen as I sing my thanks … Thank you for your love, thank you for your faithfulness'" (Psalm 138:1-2, The Msg.)*. Our Lord is the source and the recipient of thankworthy praise!

MOONBEAMS

"The sun has one kind of splendor, the moon another and the stars another" (1 Corinthians 15:41).

The surprising advantage of living near or visiting a body of water is that whatever action occurs in the sky above—rainbows, storm clouds, or sunsets—reflects into the mirror calm waters below. Because the two images can be so identical, one might wonder which scene is authentic and which one is the replica.

At times we perceive we are witnessing the hand of God dipping a brush in His palette of heavenly colors, painting a panoramic view right before our eyes. The Creator pleasures us with simultaneous views in the sky and in the water: a tranquil sky with dancing, fluffy clouds pierced by a flock of migrating geese; slices of arrow-shaped lightning bolts dividing black thunderheads; a double rainbow that weaves its arc among tall trees. God creates shadows and reflections, using variations of light, which He spoke into existence at creation when the earth was shrouded in complete darkness.

"God made two great lights—the greater light to govern the day and the lesser light to govern the night. He also made the stars.

God set them in the vault of the sky to give light on the earth, to govern the day and the night, and to separate light from darkness" *(Genesis 1:16-18).*

In the eerie shadows of a late autumn evening, the full moon birthed a celestial reflection of its radiant yellow image in the waters below. The limpid surface was strangely still, interrupted only by random wave movement, causing the moon's impression to vacillate, alternately dividing into slithering segments, then re-uniting the quivering moonbeams into a lopsided circle.

Ushering in the duplicate full moon image was a dazzling path of moonlight superimposed on the surface of the water, extending like a bridge from one side of the cove to the other. The yellow beam shimmered as the dainty waves rippled in slow motion. Could the iridescence be moon dust directly filtered through the atmosphere from the lunar planet?

The moon reconfigured into a large, desultory ball, with segments oozing and bulging as the water gently rocked and rolled. The lake's version was impressionistic. The original symmetrical roundness of the lunar orb divided irregularly like an onion sliced in random rings. First light, then deep, dark spaces shattered the yellow circle with narrow slivers and wiggly protrusions.

Slicing through the moonlit path emerged a solitary canoeist, a black silhouetted figure in the twilight. The canoeist and his paddle were resting in the stern as the skiff floated freely in the path of the moonbeam. Perhaps the person was overwhelmed by the extravagance of the moment. Soon the craft and paddler were obscured from view, engulfed by the darkness outside the perimeter of the moonlit path.

As the full moon traveled its established orbit in space, the lake's somewhat distorted, reflected image advanced closer toward the shoreline. While I pondered the unpredictable advance of the oscillating moon replica, it disappeared from sight. The moon methodically repositioned over the horizon, concluding the nocturnal, whimsical performance of the lunar duet. Devoid of celestial light, sky and lake spontaneously merged, lowering a heavy curtain of darkness on the stage of the current night's performance.

Oh, how glorious is our Lord, who splashes His brilliant designs throughout the world! He choreographs the change of seasons and pops flowers from underground to bloom in elegant beauty. He crowns majestic mountaintops with melting snow, renewing streams and ponds below. Expansive canyons are formed when God carves out great chunks of earth. He controls the ocean's waves by adjusting the rhythmic tug of the moon. How splendid is God's name and greatly to be praised!

SINK LIKE A ROCK; FLOAT LIKE A CORK

S ome of us have experienced the rare, but embarrassing situation of borrowing an item and witnessing it break while in our possession. The damage must be reported and restitution made. Though all sensible brain cells scream caution when contemplating borrowing, convenience usually nullifies any reservations we may have originally considered. *"The borrower is servant to the lender" (Proverbs 22:7b, NLT).*

Borrowing tools in not a new concept. The Old Testament prophet, Elisha, was a popular teacher in a theological seminary where young prophets were educated. The students who lived in an overcrowded dormitory invited Elisha to help them construct more living and classroom space. Each man felled a tree by the Jordan River to use in the building project. *"As one of them was cutting a tree, his ax head fell into the river. 'Oh, sir!' he cried, 'It was a borrowed ax!'" (2 Kings 6:5, NLT).*

Iron implements were rare among the Israelites. Their long-time enemies, the Philistines, controlled iron production, making the number of iron tools or weapons possessed by the Israelites pre-cious and few. *"So on the day of battle none of the people of Israel had a sword or spear, except for Saul and Jonathan" (1 Samuel 13:22, NLT).* Only the king and his son possessed the most advanced personal weapons of war. All other Israelite soldiers commonly fought with bows and arrows or slingshots.

"There were no blacksmiths in the land of Israel in those days. The Philistines wouldn't allow them for fear they would make swords and spears for the Hebrews. So whenever the Israelites needed to sharpen their plowshares, picks, axes, or sickles, they had to take them to a Philistine blacksmith" (1 Samuel 13:19-20, NLT). The price was exorbitant for sharpening farm implements. Maintaining such control allowed Israel's enemy to discern the amount and condition of equipment available, placing Israel in a vulnerable military position.

When the heavy iron ax head plunged into the river, the borrower responded in horror. He instinctively knew the value of the tool which he would be responsible for replacing or reimbursing. Since he was a student with little income, he could be facing the prospect of becoming a bondservant until he worked off his debt. Imagine the chilling fear and guilt swirling around the borrower's mind.

The prophet, Elisha, was also aware of the ramification of the lost tool. *"'Where did it fall?' the man of God asked. When he showed him the place, Elisha cut a stick and threw it into the water at that spot. Then the ax floated to the surface. 'Grab it,' Elisha said. And the man reached out his hand and grabbed it" (2 Kings 6:6-7, NLT).*

It was truly a miracle for a weighty iron ax head lying on the bottom of the muddy Jordan River to float to the surface like a buoyant cork. What wonder and gratitude Elisha's students learned outside of the classroom that day, as God provided His mercy for the welfare of His kingdom workers.

The ax head incident preserved in God's Word assures us that our Lord is personally involved in our lives without reservations. It doesn't matter how minor the problems, God always responds to our crises. He hears our prayers instantly, already aware of our personal needs before we utter the words. Included in His instructions to His disciples about prayer, Jesus said, *"'Your heavenly Father knows what you need before you ask him'" (Matthew 6:8)*. What comfort!

We may never panic in response to the loss of a broken ax head, but each of us can relate to similar traumatic times when we were beholden to someone, when our well-being or health depended on one decision, or when a situation occurred so quickly there was little time for thought or action. During each scenario we needed an advocate, a guide, or miracle worker—perhaps all three. God is delighted to help. He is the one solution to our multiple problems.

Our Lord desires that we remain in constant communication with Him, but He knows when events occur quickly, our prayer tongues may be tied in ineffectual knots. It is then that the Holy Spirit is available to interpret our needs and to speak for us.

Our heavenly Father extends mercy and grace through the sacrificial death of His Son, Jesus Christ, who paved the way for us to communicate with His holy Father. If we place our trust in Him, pledge to follow and serve Him, Jesus will enable us with His power, lavish us with His love and grace, and shower us with mercy, regardless of how underserving we may think we are.

Grace is one of the key attributes of God, His love in action, as He passionately shares all of His goodness with believers. *"My grace is sufficient for you, for my power is made perfect in weakness'" (2 Corinthians 12:9),* was God's response to the Apostle Paul when he pleaded for healing of a particularly bothersome physical affliction. Few servants have demonstrated their Lord's power as consistently as the Apostle Paul. God's strength provided during trials always exceeds our needs.

The story of the loose, flying, sinking, floating ax head comprises a mere seven verses in the Old Testament, but the message of God's miraculous intervention and His overwhelming mercy has inspired readers for centuries. Do not be lulled into thinking that any instance in life is too small to attract God's attention and to motivate His immediate action.

The prayers of God's people invite and assure God's response. *"'I am the Lord, the God of all mankind. Is anything too hard for me?'" (Jeremiah 32:27).* I think not.

PERILOUS POISON

T he warning, "leaves of three, let them be," is good advice when approaching unfamiliar plants. Poison ivy is a vine that possesses three potentially dangerous leaves.

Walking to school as a young girl, I detoured around a large elm tree dividing the sidewalk, with massive poison ivy vines encircling the trunk. I had heard disturbing stories of itchy skin rashes caused from contacting the toxic plant. I'd also heard it rumored that some individuals could be exposed to poison ivy without experiencing an adverse response. Each day when I walked past the prolific vines swirling the tree, I wondered which poison ivy theory applied to me. The suspense was more than my inquisitive mind could endure. One spring morning as the leaves waved seductively, my previous resolve collapsed. I tore a handful of leaves, crushed them, and rubbed fragments on every exposed area of my skin.

Children are often guilty of impetuous, irresponsible behavior, unfa-miliar with anticipating consequences for their actions. Fortunately, I was unaffected by the rubdown, concluding that I would be one of the few immune to the toxic effects of poison ivy for life. Had I possessed the courage to confess my reckless experiment, I may have learned that the first reaction to poison ivy merely exposed my immune system to the foreign substance. Then, when confronted with the tainted chemicals anytime in the future, my body would recognize the urushiol oil in the plant, and an immediate skin response would occur.

Later in my adult life, I inadvertently walked among poison ivy camouflaged in a wooded area. It wasn't long before an itchy rash developed. Poison ivy was the farthest diagnosis from my mind due to my neutral childhood experience. But, the second exposure alerted my immune system to identify the chemical, immediately triggering a reaction. By the time I sought evaluation three weeks later, the rash covered my limbs, causing such intense itching, aggressive medical intervention was required to treat the tenacious outbreak.

Urushiol oil is the noxious component of poison ivy, poison oak, and poison sumac plants. Contact with any part of the virulent plants leaves a smear of oil on skin, clothing, or gardening equipment, capable of surviving freezing temperatures, and remaining viable for years.

There are many other poisons that carry the potential for causing greater injury than toxic plants, leaving permanent scars or irreversible damage. What instills more fear than the destructive venom of a snake bite, rabies from an infected animal, or the long-term implications of Lyme disease from a tick bite? Even microscopic bacteria cause life-threatening infections.

Few of us are acquainted with the cause and effect of people poison. *"This is scary: You can tame a tiger, but you can't tame a tongue—it's never been done. The tongue runs wild, a wanton killer. With our tongues we bless God our Father; with the same tongues we curse the very men and women he made in his image. Curses and blessings out of the same mouth!" (James 3:7-10, The Msg.).* At times our tongues serve as unsuspecting muscles of destruction, betraying a confidence, leaking gossip, or spouting a lie. *"The Lord detests lying lips, but he delights in people who are trustworthy" (Proverbs 12:22).* Unlike poison ivy, the vitriol a tongue spews is not always reversible. Its toxin multiplies in catastrophic ways; no antidote is available.

An area of forest desecrated by a raging inferno is a chilling sight, killing every living thing in the vicinity. Fire annihilates, toppling giant trees, displacing wildlife, and destroying underground plant roots as it paints the surrounding environment black, the color of death. The ruinous effects of a consuming blaze cannot be reversed for decades, much the same as the irrevocable injuries caused by incendiary speech. Damage remains both in the path of a fire or in inflammatory words, frequently lost to redesign forever. *"Without wood a fire goes out; without a gossip a quarrel dies down. As charcoal to embers and as wood to fire, so is a quarrelsome person for kindling strife" (Proverbs 26:20-21).*

"Rumors are the vehicles that turn life into a demolition derby, and gossip and slander are the tracks on which they travel. The tracks of gossip and slander are paved with careless, idle chatter as well as the malicious intentional sharing of bad reports ... Having a tongue is like dynamite in our dentures—it must be reckoned with" (Joseph M. Stowell).

If I had known the potential danger of poison ivy, I would have used extreme caution identifying and avoiding the trifoliate plant. Our words function in the same manner, as treacherous as poisonous plants. If we monitor our negative emotions, admitting that anger, jealousy, and bitterness have the potential to inflict immeasurable heartache, we may hone our ability to control acerbic verbal outbursts. *"Those who consider themselves religious and yet do not keep a tight rein on their tongues deceive themselves and their religion is worthless" (James 1:26).*

Have you ever wanted to retract a comment you made in haste, but instead of apologizing, you offered the feckless excuse, "I was only thinking out loud?" Thinking is purely a mental function. Once uttered, our thoughts are transformed into words. *"The words of the reckless pierce like swords, but the tongue of the wise brings healing" (Proverbs 12:18).* Soothing, comforting words serve as a curative balm.

From the inside out—our hearts to our tongues—our inner monologues are filtered by God, who accomplishes the important task of purifying our thoughts. *"May the words of my mouth and the meditation of my heart be pleasing in your sight, Lord, my Rock and my Redeemer" (Psalm 19:14).*

DIVINE PROTECTOR

F ollowing our son's tonsil and adenoid surgery at age seven, one of his young friends presented him with a spider plant as a get-well gift. The plant was suspended from a bracket mounted on the upper window frame above his bed. It flourished in the sunshine and within months required transplanting into a larger pot.

One evening when his dad and I checked on our son before we retired, what a terrifying sight met us! Our child had thrown his bed covers off and was sleeping peacefully on his back with wet, clumpy potting soil scattered over his head and body. What dirty chaos!

When we awakened our son to check his mental status, we were satisfied he sustained no obvious damage. Piecing together the events, it was apparent the plant had grown too heavy for its support system. The bracket had pulled away from the window mount. The heavy pot fell, careened off the headboard, smashed the pot, and disgorged its contents directly onto our sleeping son. We gently brushed the clinging soil away from his face and eyes, impressing upon us just how tragic the accident could have been. A concussion or a skull fracture may have resulted had the plant pot crashed into his head instead of the headboard, only inches away.

Once we determined our son was unhurt and alert, we viewed the scene with far less panic and much more gratitude. Decades later, whenever that memory flashes onto our mental screens, we are grateful for our son's divine protection from injury. We thank God profusely for His miraculous deliverance.

Imagine how many times each day God oversees and protects our lives. There are instances when we are fully aware of God's actions to shield us from catastrophes. But what of the times when we are oblivious to God's interventions? Often we are divinely deterred from potentially perilous scenarios before they impact our lives. *"The Lord makes firm the steps of the one who delights in him; though he may stumble, he will not fall, for the Lord upholds him with his hand" (Psalm 37:23-24).*

Pharaoh refused to emancipate the Israelites who had provided four hundred years of free labor for the nation of Egypt. After Moses' repeated negotiations failed, God inflicted all of Egypt with ten increasingly horrendous plagues, while safeguarding His own people from collateral damage. God then freed the Israelites to walk away from their captors. When Pharaoh realized the ramifications of losing his entire slave workforce, he and his army pursued them. *"As Pharaoh approached, the Israelites looked up, and there were the Egyptians, marching toward them. They were terrified and cried out to the Lord" (Exodus 14:10).* The marchers were trapped between the expanse of the Red Sea before them and the Egyptian militia in the rear.

Only a few hours before, the Israelites had witnessed God's powerful hand creating disaster among the Egyptians while preserving their own lives. In spite of their disbelief, God was faithful. A million or more people walked on a dry path as God miraculously divided the Red Sea, forcing walls of water up on each side. The Egyptian army followed directly behind. Precisely when the last Hebrew reached the far shore, God returned the Red Sea to its normal configuration. Huge walls of water crashed down, sweeping Egyptian horses, chariots, and their riders beneath the sea. When the people observed God's mighty power, they placed their faith in Him, and confidence in Moses' leadership. They sang and praised God for His spectacular miracle, vowing to follow and fear Him in the future.

The Israelites were suddenly free of servitude for the first time in four centuries. God had heard their cries of oppression and He responded with miraculous emancipation that only He could orchestrate. One month had passed since their exodus from Egypt and the nations' walk through the Red Sea. *"In the desert the whole community grumbled against Moses and Aaron. The Israelites said to them, 'If only we had died by the Lord's hand in Egypt'" (Exodus 16:2-3).* They reflected on the bountiful food available in Egypt and the lack of food on their journey, accusing Moses of leading them into the desert to starve.

Although God had shielded and delivered His people, as soon as the immediate danger passed, doubt and fear transformed their grateful attitudes into bitterness. How quickly they forgot the miracles and blessings of God! Their faith was shallow; their motives selfish. How fickle we humans are, inclined to forsake God due to fear and complain to Him when faced with challenges. Yet, God is always faithful, consistently protecting and advocating for us.

The trials the Israelites endured during their wilderness walk were tests God used to determine their faith, to strengthen their trust, and to draw them close to Him with unquestionable submission and obedience. But the Israelites usually opted for the path of least resistance. They found it easier to complain than obey. Grumbling is effortless; obedience requires energy and discipline. The Apostle Paul admonishes us, *"'Do everything without grumbling or arguing'" (Philippians 2:14).*

We may resemble the ungrateful Israelites more than we care to admit. When was the last time you glorified God for His specific and constant protection? Is one of your first responses to thank Him for shielding you from danger or narrowly avoiding an accident? Let us praise Him for spiritual prosperity and physical safety.

"'I will take refuge in the shadow of your wings until the disaster has passed'" (Psalm 57:1). David wrote Psalm 57 while sequestered in a cave, hiding from King Saul's murderous intents. Perhaps inside, tucked within the crevice of a rock, David spied a bird's nest where the mother's protective instincts shielded her offspring beneath her wings. The avian life may have inspired David's metaphor, illustrating God's guardianship of His children with power and protection.

God grants strength during trials, not immunity that spares them from happening, exalting His glory and splendor during victories. In His shielding sanctuary, the Lord is our refuge and fortress. Snuggle beneath God's protective wings in your time of need. What a privilege, to be sheltered by Almighty God!

ULTIMATE STRENGTH

I will admit, I'm a pushover for statuesque oriental lilies. From each underground bulb, a gallant plant emerges. Growing to heights of eight feet, the lily boasts a sturdy, but invisibly reinforced stalk, whose purpose is to support and nurture the entire plant, showcasing the lily flowers it produces.

The lily plant is tall and grandiose, built for endurance, rimmed with pendulous flowers that remain stable under adverse conditions. The balanced lily stalk likely possesses specialized fibers that offer reinforcement. God, the Creator, designed the majestic lily plant for beauty and dependability, providing equilibrium by strengthening its internal composition.

What augmented inner support do we depend upon when adverse conditions assail our lives? With personal tragedy, every fiber of our being revolts, thrashing our hearts, twisting and churning our minds, and interrupting our ability to remain calm and composed. We may groan and bend under the emotional or physical weight of the hardship. *"He {God} gives strength to the weary and increases the power of the weak" (Isaiah 40:29).*

Whether we break or rebound depends upon our strength within, though personal tenacity alone is insufficient to fight our battles or to provide confidence and composure amidst life's entanglements. When the winds of adversity blow through fragile lives, our resolve may wither and snap. Though we may tremble from physical or mental weakness, there is immeasurable reinforcement available to us. God promises to convert our quivering fear to peace and our fading weakness to strength. Only then are we assured of a sufficient amount of fortitude for each trial we face.

Unlike the lily plant, our Lord designed His children with limited stamina and perseverance. The Creator implanted our psyche with innate fortitude, but when that resource of inner strength wanes, our Lord is delighted to buttress our supply with his own invincible power and potency. *"It is God who arms me with strength and keeps my way secure. (2 Samuel 22:33).*

It was a traumatic jolt the day King Jehoshaphat of Judah was informed that a coalition of enemy armies was poised outside his country's border, threatening to attack. Vulnerable without a militia or armaments, where would the king find strength to oppose such a formidable foe? *"Alarmed, Jehoshaphat resolved to inquire of the Lord …. The people of Judah came together to seek help from the Lord; indeed, they came from every town of Judah to seek him"* (2 Chronicles 20:3-4). The citizens prayed continually as they stood firm to wait for the deliverance they knew the Lord would provide. *"'For we have no power to face this vast army that is attacking us. We do not know what to do, but our eyes are on you'"* (v. 12). Delighted with their faith, God informed King Jehoshaphat and the people that they need not fight the battle, instructing them to *"'stand firm and see the deliverance the Lord will give you'" (v. 17).*

God developed unique war strategy, instigating ambushes among the foreign armies to destroy one another in the confusion of battle. No Israelite was harmed. No invading soldier survived. God's strength was magnified, and the people learned a significant lesson about faith and trust at a time when their personal supply was impoverished. *"The fear of God came on all the surrounding kingdoms when they heard how the Lord had fought against the enemies of Israel. And the kingdom of Jehoshaphat was at peace, for his God had given him rest on every side (vv. 29-30).*

Believing in God's absolute authority and power is much more straightforward when our days are peaceful and predictable. How do we respond in an emergency?

Scripture reminds us to plunge our roots of faith into the Lord's inexhaustible well of sovereign strength. We are created with a natural desire to seek God, requesting His ability to intercede in both minor and major situations. Then on the occasion when we are confronted with an unsolvable adversity, it will be our natural first response to call on God for His expertise in fighting the battle; for lavishing His gifts of peace and comfort; for His intervention to deliver a miraculous boost of strength to gain the victory He promises. *"I will strengthen you and help you; I will uphold you with my righteous right hand'" (Isaiah 41:10b).* God's right hand represents majestic, victorious power (Exodus 15:6).

The lily plant is strong for its size, but not impervious to destruction. Drought, insect infestations, and flooding will defoliate the plant, eliminating its source of life. The perennial is given one opportunity during the summer to perform superbly with nourishment stored within its bulb. If the stress is too great, the plant will collapse.

Accessing abundant spiritual blessings, Christians steadily mature in a their faith walk, combat stress, and benefit from all interactions with our heavenly Father. Whatever we lack for life and fellowship with God, He graciously provides. Union with the living, exalted Christ is the secret to contentment and the origin of abiding strength.

BUSY BODIES

To qualify that we live in a society comprised of busy people is an understatement of major proportions. Frantic to the point of distraction may be a more appropriate consequence of the activities that crowd our lives. We are proficient at multi-tasking. Dates on our calendars are filled months in advance. We are slaves of the ever-ticking clock, attuned to a shrieking alarm each morning. We are tethered to a cell phone and addicted to texting, both alerting us to instant updates of personal and newsworthy nature.

Whether we tap our toes to the beat of music or a rocket engineer calculates the exact orbit of a space shuttle, we function in a time-space perimeter. Work weeks are identified by specific hours. The world is divided into established time zones. Multiple time pieces line airport walls, identifying current hours for each country on an international scale. Clocks and calendars are integral components of our daily lives.

Do we feel the stranglehold of time commitments threatening loss of control, like a vehicle's failing brakes? We are finite beings; our time is limited, prompting us to use every hour to its full advantage. *"Be very careful, then, how you live—not as unwise but as wise, making the most of every opportunity" (Ephesians 5:15-16)*. We are instructed to walk paths of spiritual wisdom, looking toward Jesus, revealing the urgency of time and the necessity of obediently serving Him each day.

Have you ever wondered how God manages His time? He maintains the solar system, answers incessant prayers, solves myriad crises, assigns angels to divine message delivery, interacts with believers, fulfills prophesies, and restrains Satan, just a smattering of our Lord's functions. God is bound to neither clock nor calendar, exclusively human devices. *"With the Lord a day is like a thousand years, and a thousand years are like a day" (2 Peter 3:8)*. God has an eternity behind Him and another in the future. Why should He hurry? Though our Lord could have created the world within seconds by merely issuing a decree, He purposely savored the experience, accomplishing miraculous handiwork each day for a week.

Our heavenly Father is patient with His children, delaying future prophesied events to provide the opportunity for everyone, everywhere, to come to know Jesus personally. The disciple, Peter, taught, *"'Remember, our Lord's patience gives people time to be saved'" (2 Peter 3:15, NLT)*. God is long-suffering, mercifully waiting for all people to respond to His invitation to live with Him eternally.

Do we envision our prayers stacked up in a heavenly e-mail file, waiting for God to read in chronological order? *"Before a word is on my tongue you, Lord, know it completely. For you created my inmost being; you knit me together in my mother's womb. Your eyes saw my unformed body; all the days ordained for me were written in your book before one of them came to be" (Psalm 139:4,*

13, 16). Our Creator knew each of us before we were born, He designed each individual, attentive to the development of each microscopic cell in utero. God has full access to our thoughts and their intent, knowledgeable of the words we will say before our tongues utter them.

Our Lord is infinite. He existed in eternity past and He will live forevermore. There is no need for Him to count minutes or days, for He alone created time and matter. Our heavenly Father engineered, created, and now maintains the entire universe. He accomplishes everything with patient purpose. Our Lord is immutable, not subject to change. His character is inconsistent with errors, displaying only purity and holiness. We are commanded, *"Be holy because I am holy" (1 Peter 1:16).* We are instructed to be separated from sin and impurity and devoted to God.

Since we aren't going to change our time-oriented world, how can we attain a more God-like approach to daily life? *"Rejoice always, pray continually, give thanks in all circumstances; for this is God's will for you in Christ Jesus" (1 Thessalonians 5:16-18).*

In our time-space framework, we confront limits. Because we are finite, we must be cognizant of clocks and calendars to responsibly manage our predetermined amount of time each day. Only God is infinite, with no restraints to His presence or His person. He is timeless and eternal, the immortal guardian of our souls; the one in whom we are commanded to confidently place our trust.

It is impossible for mortal minds to grasp the concept of timelessness. Eternity is not an abstract term that describes a place somewhere out in the fuzzy hereafter. Eternal is a Person who was incarnated to live among us on earth. The Son of God person-ifies His Father's faithfulness and trustworthiness. Jesus Christ is eternal: He has no beginning and no end. As co-heirs with Christ, believers inherit the gift of eternal life that our Savior sacrificially earned for us on the cross of Calvary.

When Jesus appeared to His disciples after He arose from the dead, His resurrection body was constrained neither by time nor travel, by walls or doors. He appeared and disappeared at will. When we live eternally with our Savior in heaven, time-space limits we now experience will cease; not a clock or a calendar will be found. What a magnificent reward heaven will be for believers currently bound by finite obstacles!

King David wrote Psalm 31 during terrifying times. His conspiring enemies used such extreme intimidation tactics, even the King's friends were persuaded to abandon him. David resolved, *"But I trust in you, Lord. You are my God. My times are in your hands'"* *(Psalm 31:14-15)*. Like David, do we place our time and our lives in the Almighty's capable hands, with unwavering trust, relinquishing nefarious foes and unknown forces to God's power, relying implic-itly on His faithfulness? Earthly time produces significant conse-quences when God's characteristics permeate our lives. Readily accept the reputation as a busy body for Christ!

DOUBTING THOMAS?

O n the first Easter Sunday evening, Jesus' disciples were gathered behind locked doors, fearing retaliation by the Jewish rulers, when their Master suddenly appeared in His glorified body and greeted them. Initially the disciples were so terrified they were paralyzed with fear, thinking Jesus was a ghost. But Jesus reassured them: *"'Why are you troubled and why do doubts rise in your minds? Look at my hands and my feet. It is I myself! Touch me and see; a ghost does not have flesh and bones, as you see I have'. When he had said this, he showed them his hands and feet. And while they still did not believe it because of joy and amazement, he asked them, 'Do you have anything to eat?' They gave him a piece of broiled fish and he took it and ate it in their presence"* (Luke 24:38-43), demonstrating that He had a functioning human body that required food.

The disciple Thomas was absent from the group on Resurrection Sunday. When his fellow disciples relayed to Thomas, *"'We have seen the Lord!'"* Thomas replied, *"'Unless I see the nail marks in his hands and put my finger where the nails were, and put my hand into his side, I will not believe'"* (John 20:25). The following week when Thomas was gathered with the disciples, Jesus again appeared to them through locked doors, then focused His atten-tion on Thomas. *"'Put your finger here; see my hands. Reach out your hand and put it into my side. Stop doubting and believe'"* (v. 27).* Jesus was patient and merciful to permit Thomas the same opportunity to feel His scars as He had provided the other disciples the previous week. Immediately, Thomas proclaimed a climactic confession: *"'My Lord and my God!'"* (v.28).*

We have no indication that Thomas touched his Lord's wounds. It wasn't necessary. Thomas instantly recognized his Master—His voice, His authority, His love. Our Savior tenderly and compassion-ately meets the honest doubts of all believers. As with Thomas, Jesus willingly provides proof without criticism. Following a period of doubt in our lives, we are often led to new spiritual enlighten-ment. *"Let us draw near to God with a sincere heart and with the full assurance that faith brings"* (Hebrews 10:22). God is compas-sionate toward a believer who seeks the knowledge and help only He can fulfill. His resources are unlimited; His love unfathomable.

Faith involves submission, humility, and an open mind of belief in our Lord alone. *"'These are the ones I look on with favor; those who are humble and contrite in spirit and who tremble at my word'"* *(Isaiah 66:2).* God is a friend of believers, and He desires that we communicate with Him in that capacity. Are your prayers as natural with Jesus as conversation with an earthly friend? Our relationship with our Lord must be forthright and sincere, with hearts con-sistently abiding in Him, requesting God's guidance and wisdom, absolutely convinced He will respond. *"But when you ask, you must believe and not doubt, because the one who doubts is like a wave of the sea, blown and tossed by the wind. That person should not*

expect to receive anything from the Lord. Such a person is dou-
ble-minded and unstable in all they do" (James 1:6-7). The nautical
comparison evokes images of a believer tossed by waves of doubt
on an open sea of confusion.

For centuries Thomas has been encumbered with an unmerited
moniker as if he were the only doubter in history. Incredibly, there
is an entry in contemporary dictionaries for "doubting Thomas,"
defined as an habitually doubtful person. Nowhere in God's Word
is Thomas identified as a repetitive doubter. There is only one incident when Thomas sought confirmation that Jesus was the risen
Lord, the same evidence afforded the other disciples a week earlier.
Jesus didn't rebuke His disciple, but patiently and lovingly offered
Thomas the proof he was seeking.

Every life is more significant than to reduce the sum of it to one
experience. History has judged Thomas harshly and permanently.
It causes me to wonder the reason Thomas was specifically sin-
gled out as a skeptic, when the doubt and unbelief of other char-
acters in God's Word had far-reaching consequences. Would any
of us appreciate having our lives defined by one lapse of faith?
God's lack of spiritual censure of Thomas assures us of His mercy
and understanding.

Zachariah and Elizabeth were childless, a major disappointment
in their lives and particularly disgraceful for a Hebrew woman.
One day while Zachariah was performing his priestly duties at the
temple, an angel appeared. *"'Your prayer has been heard. Your*
wife Elizabeth will bear you a son, and you are to call him John ...
He will be great in the sight of the Lord.' Zachariah asked the angel,

'How can I be sure of this? I am an old man and my wife is well along in years'" (Luke 1:13, 15a, 18). Although the angel had been sent as God's messenger from heaven promising the most fabulous gift of his lifetime, Zachariah wanted more proof. At that moment, disbelief overshadowed his trust. Thus, the angel struck Zachariah mute *"Because you did not believe my words, which will come true at their appointed time'" (v. 20)*. The future father was temporarily punished for his unbelief. Distrust is blind and dumb, as illustrated by Zachariah's lack of verbal communication until the day of John's birth. Zachariah, a priest who daily prayed at the altar of God for a child, questioned whether God's answer was reliable.

Do we ever pray as Zachariah did, asking God for something specific, but not fully believing our request will be answered? Let us reflect on our heart's conviction before we pray, to ascertain if we possess tenacious faith anchored in Jesus to support the weight of our request.

Following Jesus' ascension, Thomas, like the other disciples, took the Good News of the Gospel into the known world of his time. With courage and conviction, Thomas planted churches in India, establishing Christianity that still survives today in a predominantly Hindu country. There he was martyred. We owe a great deal to Thomas, who teaches believers by example that Jesus is not threatened by our sincere questions. He welcomes honest, searching inquiries that fuel our daily journey as we reach out to touch and to be touched by Jesus' nail-scarred hands. Then we will know from experience what Jesus assured. *"See, I have engraved you on the palms of my hands'" (Isaiah 49:16)*.

SOVEREIGN ENCOUNTER

It was clear and cool as I walked the path toward the cabin in the woods. With each step I could detect the crunchy snap of exploding dry pine cones beneath my feet, the only distraction that pierced the quiet serenity of the evening. A full moon illuminated the placid freshwater lake, a picturesque scene peering through the black silhouetted pine branches at twilight.

A wispy plume of smoke emanated from the stone chimney. Without a breeze on this calm evening, the smoke lingered in a vertical spiral, suspended high above the cabin roof, producing a familiar woodsy scent permeating the surroundings.

Entering the log cabin, I was greeted by rustic ambience. A lively crackling fire filled the imposing fieldstone fireplace on the opposite wall. Fingers of heat reached out to entwine my cool body with penetrating warmth. Once my eyes adjusted to the softly glowing lights, I viewed the form of someone snuggled into a high backed chair. As I spoke softly to avoid shattering the precious silence perforated only by the sizzling of the fireplace logs, He arose to greet me. Though I had never met Him in the flesh, once we established eye contact, I readily identified the mysterious host as Jesus Christ, my Savior. Our glances locked in mutual acknowledgement. When I responded to His gesture to collapse in a nearby chair, we talked effortlessly, the manner in which best friends converse. Jesus had never been far away, for His main residence is my heart. This rare, tangible encounter in a remote location afforded us an occasion of undisturbed fellowship.

There were no uncomfortable interludes in our dialogue, only the astonishing affection of my Lord's true character. I was in the presence of the creator and sustainer of the universe, the Prince of Peace, and the Savior of my soul. Generously, Jesus was also my friend. *"You are my friends if you do what I command" (John 15:14).* Jesus accepts His friends into His confidence, just as He hospitably welcomed me this evening. Interacting with Jesus in the tranquil atmosphere reinforced His authority and adoration, purity and perfection, glory and grace.

The minute Jesus uttered my name, joy coursed through my entire being, stimulating excitement of body and soul. As He grasped my hands in His, I could palpate the still-prominent scars on His palms, created during Christ's heinous crucifixion two millenniums ago, a poignant reminder of His love and sacrifice willingly offered, opening the way for me to boldly and confidently communicate with Him at any time.

Jesus was splendid and majestic, the King of kings who fully understood my human weakness. He verbally lavished me with love and grace, instructing me to continually grow in faith. Jesus reassured me of His supreme interest in my development as His ardent follower, urging me to obey His commandments, explaining that the more I love Him, the more my love will overflow toward others.

Christ admonished me to share my interests and goals with Him, depending on His perfect plans and precise timing for answers to my prayers. He counseled me to lean on Him; to cling to Him. As I evolve closer to Jesus in fellowship, He challenges me: *"Rejoice always, pray continually, give thanks in all circumstances; for this is God's will for you in Christ Jesus"* (1 Thessalonians 5:16-18).

I didn't want our visit to end in the idyllic environment engulfed by peace and shared affection. Exuberance and hope produced from being in Christ's immediate presence renewed my mind and soul. I chose the remote cabin in the woods as the perfect retreat from the stresses of daily life. Psychologists agree that mental burdens are lessened by the act of projecting one's thoughts into a familiar, peaceful scene.

At first consideration, it would seem my vivid imagination had shifted into overdrive, but actually God transported me emotionally to the cabin in response to my earnest request. During recent Scripture memorization, the meaning of one particular verse eluded my understanding: *"Whoever dwells in the shelter of the Most High will rest in the shadow of the Almighty"* (Psalm 91:1). Since meeting with Jesus prayerfully, I now have a much greater comprehension of His teachings. Once I physically dwelled in the presence of Jesus' shelter, I felt secure resting in the shadow of His protection that penetrates every area of my life.

God desires that we seek the knowledge of His Word. Granted, His manner of revealing truths to me for memorization purposes were unusual, but I must not compare my heavenly Father's communication methods to my earthly expectations. *"'Call to me and I will answer you and tell you great and unsearchable things you do not know'" (Jeremiah 33:3).* Our prayers invite God's response.

God graciously devised the mechanism of prayer. As we talk reverently with our Lord, we may be spiritually transported to any number of unique vicinities that appeal to us individually. The cabin scene is one of unsurpassed luxury for me. Where will you go for shelter and rest to meet with your Lord? It could be as familiar as your backyard or as reminiscent as a childhood memory. The most important factors in abiding with Jesus remain our willingness and obedience to pray, connecting us to our Lord anytime, anywhere.

"Jesus told his disciples ... that they should always pray and not give up" (Luke 18:1). As we constantly share details of our lives with Jesus, we need withhold nothing from our trustworthy Lord and friend. Prayer is powerful; prayer is a privilege; prayer is conversing with the One God of the universe, who is supremely interested in every aspect of our lives. Prayer is phenomenal! Let us declare His glory as we attribute to Him the splendor and majesty He deserves. *"Look to the Lord and his strength; seek his face always" (1 Chronicles 16:11).*

GIANTS TOWER;
GRASSHOPPERS COWER

After four centuries of servitude to the Egyptians, God chose Moses to lead the nation of Israel into the Promised Land, where they would be free to own and govern their own property, rich in natural resources.

Egypt's Pharaoh was vehemently opposed to losing the entire Jewish nation of slave laborers. To convince Pharaoh, God targeted the Egyptian people with ten progressively ghastly plagues that dreadfully impacted their health and lifestyle. Pharaoh's heart remained hardened until the ultimate plague, when God slaughtered all firstborn males, including both animals and humans. In his grief, Pharaoh finally let God's people go. He could not compete with the power of God, *"Who is like you—majestic in holiness, awesome in glory, working wonders?" (Exodus 15:11).* The Lord protected Israel from each plague, leading the nation safely out of Egypt during the night of Passover.

About a million Israelites with droves of livestock marched across the desert, reaching an impasse at the Red Sea. There God divided the waters, piling up walls of the sea on each side, creating a path for the Israelites to walk through on the dry sea floor. Pharaoh, who soon reversed his decision about releasing his slave work force, followed closely behind with his massive militia in pursuit. God threw the Egyptian army into confusion, causing the wheels to fall off their chariots to slow them during the chase. When the last Israelite crossed the sea, the Lord restored the two columns of water to the sea basin, raising the sea level, swallowing the men, chariots, and horses of the entire Egyptian militia. *"That day the Lord saved Israel from the hands of the Egyptians, and Israel saw the Egyptians lying dead on the shore" (Exodus 14:30).*

God commanded His people to occupy the Promised Land, His generous gift of 300,000 square miles, land He had already surveyed and pronounced good. God promised, *"I will give into your hands the people who live in the land, and you will drive them out before you" (Exodus 23:31b).* God's people refused to trust Him, and instead, requested a scouting party. The team that would secretly research the Promised Land was composed of one man from each of the twelve tribes of Israel.

When the dozen spies returned from investigating the Promised Land, there was unanimous agreement concerning the cities, people, and produce available, but no consensus remained as to whether the Israelites could conquer the land, even though God promised to prepare the way and fight for them to defeat pockets of resistance.

Ten of the twelve spies were fixated on the giants found living in Canaan. *"'The land we explored devours those living in it. All the people we saw are of great size. We seemed like grasshoppers in our own eyes and we looked the same to them'"* (Numbers 13:32, 33b). Ten spies instilled fear among the general populace by exaggerating reports about their exploration, convinced they wouldn't be able to defeat the foreigners in battle.

Pessimistic words by the faithless spies led to mourning by the entire community, which then prompted a rebellion against God. How quickly they had forgotten the miracles God performed in Egypt. The Israelites preferred death, as expressed in their lament: *"'If only we had died in Egypt! Or in this wilderness! Why is the Lord bringing us to this land only to let us fall by the sword?'"* (Numbers 14:2).

The ten fearful spies seduced the crowd with their scare tactics, convincing the people that it would be impossible to subdue the enemy. Their defeatist attitude arose from depending on inadequate human strength. The people disobeyed God by displaying fear that suffocates trust. Believers must never dispute how God accomplishes what He promises, but acknowledge that He is always faithful to His Word.

Joshua and Caleb, the two remaining spies, were convinced that victory was possible by relying on God's promises. They encouraged the Israelite assembly with positive reports, minimizing temporary obstacles, trusting God to lead them to victory. *"'If the Lord is pleased with us, he will lead us into that land, a land flowing with milk and honey, and will give it to us. Only do not rebel against the Lord. And do not be afraid of the people of the land, because we will devour them. Their protection is gone, but the Lord is with us. Do not be afraid of them'"* (Numbers 14:8-9). When God was leading the offensive, there were no undefeatable nations.

As the Israelites soon learned, it is dangerous to disobey God. The mutinous generation was punished for unbelief. The ten spies were immediately struck down with a plague and died. Of the chosen twelve, only Caleb and Joshua were spared. The remainder of the people traveled daily, but made little progress toward the Promised Land. The entire generation was led in a circular path through the desert until their natural deaths.

The recent beneficiaries of miracles to save the nation from enslavement in Egypt quickly dismissed the power and presence of God. They possessed selfish, selective memories that sabotaged their own people's hopes and dreams. They believed tall men and fortified cities were a greater threat than God's mighty wrath. What shallow, dangerous thinking, to spurn the victory God offers! No perceived impossibility outpaces God's power.

Do you have giants that loom large in your vision, deceiving you to think that God's promises aren't sufficient? God assures you that He is able to subjugate any problem posing as a giant.

The Lord is still parting the waters of improbability to accomplish the miraculous in our lives. We have the tendency to reduce our faith to the diminutive size of a grasshopper, annoying those around us with the relentless chirping of doubts and complaints. Faith is silenced by the constant cacophony of grasshoppers. A small amount of faith creates the occasion for a giant work of God. "Focus on giants—you stumble; focus on God-your giants tumble" (Max Lucado).

DAILY MIRACLES

A magnificent glowing light emanated from a perfectly round moon beaming lemon yellow in the endless expanse of inky sky. The luminous globe was surrounded by a hazy bronze rim, like the patina of corroded metal in direct sunlight. The lunar reflection smashed into the water in a pool of illumination, snuggling up to the opposite shore of the lake. Sizzling and squirming in an interrupted jagged row of dazzling radiance, the trail of light erected a bridge of scintillating golden crossbeams spanning the cove.

A soft gust of wind tickled the limpid water as the moonbeams bounced along like a flat stone scaled across the surface, leaving a succession of shallow depressions in its wake, featuring a miracle of the senses. *"The heavens declare the glory of God; the skies proclaim the work of His hands" (Psalm 19:1).*

Driving through a densely wooded highway one November afternoon, the brilliant fall foliage surrounded me like colorful deciduous curtains draping the windows of the season. The fragile, dried hardwood leaves, splattered conspicuously with rainbow colors, loomed randomly among the green, fuzzy softwoods.

God's extravagant designs are amazing. Right before my eyes He splashed a panorama of color, proliferating beauty as far as I could see. The thick border of trees blended into one placid, but sensational, light-slathered glimpse of liquid gold in the afternoon sun. As I pondered the blazing scenery, it occurred to me the creator of all beauty, whose pleasure it is to share His handiwork, encircled me with serenity, fluently displaying His palette of brilliant colors. *"God richly provides us with everything for our enjoyment"* *(1Timothy 6:17b).*

Throughout the frigid winter, flower bulbs remain several inches below ground, frozen and dormant, storing energy and nutrition in an incongruously small package brimming with an explosive potential for life in the underground tuber. With the mere addition of water and sunshine in the warm months, the bulb bursts forth with a rapid growth of green stalks. Once the plant reaches appropriate height, the swollen blossom at the tip of the stalk unfurls. Colors gradually shade from soft chartreuse to fabulous fuchsia, emitting a sweet, exotic fragrance. What a miracle of creation! *"See how the lilies of the field grow... not even Solomon in all his splendor was dressed like one of these"* *(Matthew 6:28-29).*

We may experience a multitude of God's discernible miracles throughout our lifetime. However, we need not wait for a single extraordinary event when each new day is an exhilarating miracle of God's beauty and extravagance, love and fellowship, which He delightfully lavishes upon His children. Our heavenly Father habitually creates a panoramic sunset, entwining orange and purple clouds dancing in the evening sky, twirling hues of pink on a floor of blue, a mesmerizing array of fluid color.

Fields of deeply pigmented, swaying wildflowers project a tranquil scene in the morning sunlight, while a babbling brook tumbles over exposed boulders, chanting a barely discernible melody. Deep within the forest, wild bushes offer sumptuous fruit hanging pendulously from a labyrinth of branches, offering delights for both diminutive chipmunks and mammoth bears.

A thunderous waterfall crashes into the age-carved earth below, plunging great distances to burrow into a glassy pool of fresh mountain water. The sun reflects off water droplets, generating prisms of iridescent rainbows twittering in the foreground. Distant snow-capped mountain ranges shout the majesty of God from cloud-piercing heights. Our Lord digs sculptured canyons deep within the earth's crust, whispers wind through the trees, and manipulates the direction of ocean tides with the moon He suspends in space.

Life itself is a tangible miracle, every day a visual smorgasbord. We need only open our hearts to recognize the prolific gifts of God. He loves us monumentally, expressing His intimacy by continually interacting in our lives. God's glory shines resplendent as beauty proliferates in His presence. What a continuous, splendiferous miracle made for you by the creator of the entire universe, your personal, powerful God!

"This is the day the Lord has made; let us rejoice and be glad in it" (Psalm 118:24).

LIVING WATER

W ithin the hush of the dense forest, jealously guarded and protected by those apprised of its location, resides a quietly bubbling spring of water purified through a naturally deep layer of fine, white oscillating sand. The water percolates from a destination below ground level. Camp owners in the vicinity have constructed a three-sided wooden hut that shields the pristine water from falling tree debris. The front of the rustic building is exposed, allowing access to dip the fresh, gurgling water.

As I stand encompassed by a colorful canopy of rattling autumn foliage, I detect the subtle murmuring of spring water regurgitating through sifting sand, slowly overflowing and trickling into an adjoining brook. I'm mentally transported to the scene in Samaria where a local woman met Jesus at the town well during the noonday heat. She carried large pots to fill with her family's daily water supply, when Jesus, parched after a long journey and resting at the well, asked her to dip water for Him. As they conversed, Jesus explained the gift of Living Water as the flowing, constantly replenished reservoir within Himself, as from a spring or a mountain stream that revives and refreshes life, not stagnant water like that from a cistern. His Living Water invigorates body and soul.

When the Samaritan woman asked Jesus where to procure such Living Water, *"Jesus said, 'Everyone who drinks this water will get thirsty again and again. Anyone who drinks the water I give will never thirst—not ever. The water I give will be an artesian spring within, gushing fountains of endless life'"* (John 4:13-14, The Msg.). Little did the Samaritan woman suspect she would ever meet a source of Living Water; those who partake spiritually never thirst again. She couldn't grasp the concept until Jesus contrasted His pure, satisfying water to the desperate yearnings of the human soul. Jesus is the wellspring of life. One drop of Living Water on a languishing heart improves the parched condition eternally. Once you've sipped Jesus' pure water, the contaminated tap water of life will no longer provide appeal.

Do we find the love of Jesus, His gift of abundant life on earth, and His promise of eternal life as spiritually satisfying as a drink of spring water quenches our physical thirst? *"As the deer pants for streams of water, so my soul pants for you, my God. My soul thirsts for God, for the living God"* (Psalm 42:1-2). A deer, its hide frothing with sweat from an exhausting run through the forest, approaches a stream, panting in anticipation of gulps of pure mountain water. As our hearts pant for the healing powers of Living Water, we are propelled to the fountainhead—Jesus

Like deer of the forest yearn for water, our faith responds by longing for God's presence. Jesus is our confidence as we enjoy His gift of life to the fullest on this earth, and His enduring promise of eternity with Him in heaven. *"All who have this hope in him purifies himself, just as he is pure"* (1 John 3:3). Similar to the deer in crisis, we've had periods in our lives when the need for a drink was paramount, when we've felt parched, suffering from some degree of dehydration. At times, when our mouths detect the need for liquid, our hearts pant for the healing powers of Living Water.

The spiritual gifts to which we inwardly and outwardly aspire, those which completely amaze and satisfy, abide in the person of Living Water, as Jesus replenishes, regenerates, and reinvigorates our lives. If we crave pure drinking water to satisfy our physical thirst, how much more we desire Living Water to fulfill us spiritually. Our needs for life are found in Jesus, the giver of all blessings. He is our everlasting supply of supremacy and sovereignty, perfection and purity. He is the Bread of Life and the spring of Living Water to sustain us; the root of all strength to empower us; the gift of redemption poured out for eternal life.

The prophet, Jeremiah, records God's accusation of His disobedient people: *"'My people have committed two sins: They have forsaken me, the spring of living water, and have dug their own cisterns, broken cisterns that cannot hold water'" (Jeremiah 2:13).* Cracked, leaking vessels, inadequate to contain a predictable amount of water, are compared to worthless idols, which will frustrate their worshippers. By contrast, the living God is unlimited in resources, the wellspring of abundant and satisfying life for His followers.

Let us call on God to supply our vital physical, emotional, and spiritual provisions. His qualities flow infinitely deep. There is no one more steadfast, sinless, or splendid than our Savior. Tap into Christ's resources, which He willingly offered the Samaritan woman at the well. *"Blessed are those who trust in the Lord and have made the Lord their hope and confidence. They are like trees planted along a riverbank, with roots that reach deep into the water. Such trees are not bothered by the heat or worried by long months of drought. Their leaves stay green, and they never stop producing fruit"* (Jeremiah 17:7-8, NLT). The Lord is our constant source of pure, refreshing water; the origin of life overflowing.

Unlike the clear, pure water that bubbles continually from the natural forest spring, Jesus is our source of Living Water, proficient at permanently quenching our heart's thirst. There is no secret location or the need to walk a distance to obtain Living Water, for Jesus urges us to call on Him anytime for a supernatural, perpetual supply of abundant blessings.

WHOLEHEARTED FAITH

W hen Scripture refers to the heart, it does not allude to the muscular pump located in one's left chest. The heart/soul symbolizes our intellectual, moral, and emotional control-central. It contains personality; shelters memory, love, and the longing for God. Our soul is identified as the invisible psyche where Jesus abides, the only part of a believer transported to heaven immediately following physical death.

In modern times our hearts are described as the epicenter of our emotions and worship. Jesus knows the thoughts and motives harbored there, discerning whether we are wholeheartedly devoted to Him, hardhearted unbelievers, or indifferent to His love and sacrifice. King David's instructions passed on to his son, Solomon, are still pertinent to us: *"Acknowledge the God of your father, and serve him with wholehearted devotion and with a willing mind, for the Lord searches every heart and understands every desire and every thought. If you seek him he will be found by you " (1 Chronicles 28:9).* God is involved in the heart affairs of our lives, far more interested in the inner characteristics of a follower of Christ than with outward features.

"Amaziah was twenty-five years old when he became king. He did what was right in the eyes of the Lord, but not wholeheartedly" (2 Chronicles 25:1a, 2). Amaziah initially manifested obedience toward the Lord, but on one occasion, after conquering a pagan country, he purposely carried their enemy's idol gods home to worship. *"He set them up as his own gods, bowed down to them and burned sacrifices to them. The anger of the Lord burned against Amaziah"* (2 Chronicles 25:14).

King Amaziah began his twenty-nine year reign with zeal and determination to uphold God's laws, serving Him without reservation. However, during the course of the king's long career, he suffered gradual loss of commitment to his Lord and his people. Self-sufficiency and greed compromised unreserved devotion. He no longer possessed intense singleminded devoutness for leading a nation with God as his priority and guide.

To serve God wholeheartedly is to express in thought or action, in the most exuberant but determined way, a vital commitment to walk with our Lord. Jesus commanded, *"'Love the Lord your God with all your passion and prayer and muscle and intelligence— and love your neighbor as well as you do yourself'"* (Luke 10:27, The Msg.).

What do our individual lives disclose about our hearts' focus? Does passion fuel our worship? Exhilarating joy bursts into wholehearted service when we are committed exclusively to our Lord Jesus Christ. He gave His life as the ultimate gift to redeem our sins and to secure eternal life for believers. Jesus expects a wholehearted relationship of absolute devotion, intense love, and unmitigated obedience. He then extends to us dynamic power to follow His commandments.

Caleb was one of twelve Israelite men chosen for a fact-finding mission to the Promised Land. Upon their return, ten of the spies claimed exaggerated details, intending to evoke fear among the population. Caleb and Joshua presented realistic, encouraging information, asking the people to depend upon God's power to lead them into triumphant victory in the new land. *"God said, 'Because my servant Caleb has a different spirit and follows me wholeheartedly, I will bring him into the land he went to, and his descendants will inherit it'" (Numbers 14:24).*

Many parents instruct their children from an early age to do a job well or not do it at all. If secular teaching devalues half-hearted efforts, love and service for our Lord must attain a much higher standard. *"Whatever you do, whether in word or deed, do it all in the name of the Lord Jesus, giving thanks to God the Father through him" (Colossians 3:17).*

Rejection of God was exemplified by the Pharaoh of Egypt when Moses negotiated release of the nation of Israel from centuries of slavery. God devised ten horrific plagues affecting every aspect of the Egyptians' lives. With each increasingly ugly plague, Pharaoh weakened his resolve to let God's people go. Finally he begged Moses to appeal to God to discontinue the most current plague. Exhibiting patience and mercy, God granted Pharaoh's request. But, when Pharaoh witnessed relief from the plagues, he regressed into his old pattern of an unyielding hard heart, ultimately refusing to permit the Israelites to travel. Pharaoh revealed a consistently sinful life of unbelief, dispassion, and bitterness.

Hardheartedness signifies refusal to take God and His Word seriously. Pharaoh's heart was solidified by his own deceit. Later, God hardened Pharaoh's heart permanently to accomplish His purpose of releasing His children from slavery. If it had been available in Pharaoh's lifetime, his ECG would have revealed a straight line of apathy and death.

Suppose your name and life accomplishments were included in Scripture, exposed for all generations to read. Would God declare you steadfastly devoted to Him? Or, would He clarify, as He did for King Amaziah, that you did right in His eyes, but not wholeheartedly? There are times in life when we display eager enthusiasm, animated commitment, or intense thirst. We love a spouse wholeheartedly; we often pursue a hobby with dedication; we may thirst for knowledge. Most of us would accept a financial windfall with overwhelming ecstasy.

Why do we apply earnest devotion to our physical/mental endeavors, but ignore commitment in spiritual relationships? Jesus desires that we open our hearts as His residence, motivating us to proclaim complete trust and zeal toward Him. Our relationship then becomes an indisputable witness to the world that we are passionate about serving Christ wholeheartedly. Let us perfect our spiritual health, glorifying Jesus by serving Him wholeheartedly.

"So if you're serious about living this new resurrection life with Christ, act like it. Pursue the things over which Christ presides. Don't

shuffle along, eyes to the ground, absorbed with the things right in front of you. Look up, and be alert to what is going on around Christ—that's where the action is. See things from his perspective." *(Colossians 3:1-2, The Msg.).* Faith is a wholehearted affair!

QUELL LIFE'S STORMS

As a child I secretly yearned for my name to be assigned to a hurricane. Recently the Weather Channel flashed devastating scenes on TV of Hurricane Patricia, a category V storm. My anticipated childhood longing was replaced by an adult reaction of horror that my name was associated with massive destruction, death, and human suffering on all levels.

Hurricane Patricia gained landfall in Mexico, ripped down mountainsides, and pulled whole chunks of earth and trees into an escalating mudslide that tore through sparsely populated, remote villages. In Texas and adjoining states, phenomenal amounts of raging rain and wind buried vehicles in rising street floods. People young and old awaited rescue as they tenaciously clung to rooftops and tall trees. Vehement currents snagged possessions, swirling them downstream in the rushing, turbulent waters to deposit miles away.

Victims who perilously hover between life and death are more willing to compromise objects of trust. Normally, those who are disinterested in parachuting as a recreational sport, decline participating when the opportunity is offered. During an emergency, when life is threatened by rising flood waters, fear is cancelled by the intense instinct to escape drowning by any method, even if it involves suspension in a safety harness from a rescue helicopter.

Someone who has previously suffered a memorable bout of sea-sickness would likely refuse a pleasure ride in any watercraft. When the only option of surviving a flood is transport by boat to dry land, accepting temporary seasickness from a boat ride over the permanence of death is inherent. During such trials, fear evolves into hesitant trust. Stretched to the maximum and modified for self-preservation, trust is often redefined to accommodate catastrophes.

In any crisis, trust communicated by helping strangers is heartfelt. Humbling lessons can be learned from an extended hand thrust in the victim's direction. The rescuer reveals a willingness to aid by direct eye contact, eager body language, and clarity of directions. The endangered person reciprocates by explicitly complying to instructions. Prejudice and fear diminish when recovery is a collaborative effort.

When Jesus and His disciples were deluged with long days spent teaching and healing, they retreated by boat, affording solitude on the Sea of Galilee. One night as the boat sailed toward the far shore in a menacing storm, Jesus slept in the stern. The disciples were terrified of the violent waves sloshing over the gunnels, nearly capsizing the craft, flooding their thoughts with fears of perishing at sea.

With the boat nearly swamped, *"The disciples woke him {Jesus}
and said to him, 'Teacher, don't you care if we drown?' He got up,
rebuked the wind and said to the waves, 'Quiet! Be still!' Then the
wind died down and it was completely calm" (Mark 4:38-39).* Jesus'
authority over the elements of nature was revealed when the wind
and waves immediately obeyed His commands, further affirming
to the disciples that He was the Son of God. The disciples were
awe-struck by their Master's supremacy, whose power exceeded
that of the raging sea. They were shocked that Jesus silenced the
storm; the waves obeyed with immediate tranquility.

In a world where self-reliance is embraced, are we depending
solely on our own meager strength to save and sustain us? When
the next storm of life reveals its wrath—a destructive hurricane,
diagnosis of cancer, delivery of devastating news—do we feel ade-
quately prepared with the emotional stamina to respond to such
major crises? When the paltry strength we amass to confront turmoil is depleted, weakness fills the void.

Almighty God is our only adequate source of power and strength.
He is willing and waiting for us to call on Him. The Lord assures
us, *"'So do not fear, for I am with you; do not be dismayed, for I
am your God. I will strengthen you and help you; I will uphold you
with my righteous right hand'" (Isaiah 41:10).* God, who encourages boldness and persistence in prayer, is delighted to convert our
diminishing weakness to His remarkable strength. However, God
neither crowds nor coerces. He created each of us with self-will
and He patiently awaits our decisions to trust in His ability to calm
the myriad squalls threatening daily existence.

Storms of life possess the potential to diminish peace. Are you prepared with the conviction that, come what may, your trust is indelibly anchored in Christ, as you steadfastly cling to His power? Don't wait for the next emergency. Be prepared. Seek God in prayer. Develop a personal relationship with God that functions perpetually. Your heavenly Father has been waiting for you to call on Him as Lord and Savior. When you submit to Him, there will be no limit to the power, protection, and peace with which He lavishes you.

When the water crashed over the sides of the disciples' boat, they were temporarily incapacitated, unable to focus or function; doubt and confusion prevailed. To prevent such oppressive reactions, lean hard on Jesus. Request that He accompany and guide you on every excursion of life. Christ is the only one in whom to resolutely place your trust for all of the minor and major problems that assail. *"Trust in the Lord with all your heart and do not depend on your own understanding. Seek his will in all you do, and he will show you which path to take" (Proverbs 3:5-6, NLT).* To rely solely on one's own mastery of life generates pride and hinders trust. Humility and obedience activate God's powerful promises. To know God intimately is to trust Him with emphatic devotion.

I have re-evaluated my adolescent desire for name recognition, preferring to sink into obscurity from future storm notoriety. As for impending dangers, my Lord is masterfully adept at quelling all of my storms.

WORRYWART OR WORRY NOT

As recorded in the Old Testament, Abraham and Sarah lived in the advanced civilization in Ur of the Chaldeans when God commanded them to leave their home, family, and friends to follow Him. They unhesitatingly obeyed God by traveling to an unknown land for an unspecified period of time, giving up all things familiar for an obscure future (Genesis 12:1-9).

The couple worshipped God faithfully and He blessed them with wealth, calculated by expansive land holdings and burgeoning animal herds. God himself was Abraham's greatest treasure. Although the Lord promised further greatness, Abraham questioned what God could possibly give him of value, since he had no heir to his estate. What Abraham and Sarah desired most was a son, but Sarah had remained barren all of her life. God then promised the couple an heir and descendants as numerous as the stars in the sky and sand on the seashore.

Both Abraham and Sarah were aging. Abraham was eighty-five years old; Sarah, seventy-five. Years passed without the awaited child. Did they doubt God's sincerity? Though the Bible account doesn't specify, we assume from their actions, both fear and disbelief were involved. Speculating that God had forgotten His covenant, the marriage partners decided to take matters into their own hands. Abraham fathered a son, Ishmael, with Sarah's maidservant, Hagar. Such an arrangement was acceptable in their society for the purpose of producing a male heir, but Abraham and Sarah knowingly disobeyed God's higher law.

When Abraham was one hundred years old and Sarah ninety, angels visited, announcing that Sarah would give birth to their own son within a year. It had been fifteen years since the initial pledge, sufficient time to wonder how, when, or if God's prophecy would come to fruition. The Lord's characteristics of purity and holiness made it impossible for God to renege on His oath. It was important the couple learn that their Lord was unequivocally faithful. When God's vow materialized, all details were fulfilled exactly as He had originally promised. Because the couple had irresponsibly implemented their own plan by ignoring God's covenant, there were consequences. Animosity arose between the two sons, Isaac and Ishmael, extending to all future generations of their descendants, the Israelites and the Arabs. Relationships between the two nations remain hostile to this day.

Formidable situations are typically laced with fear and apprehension, debilitating anxiety, and a worrisome focus. Expressed by one pundit, worry is useless. "If you worry that a bad thing is going to happen, and then it does, you've been through it twice." Who wants double trouble? Most of us practice discipline in areas affecting our health, and yet we implement worry, a health wrecking ball. Anxiety compromises our physical, emotional, and spiritual well-being, displacing the abundant peace God offers.

Worship and worry are mutually exclusive, repelling like similar poles of a magnet. Worry is a spiritual handicap that casts doubt on the sincerity of our Christian faith. If we profess to trust our loving God, who perfectly plans every aspect of our lives, but we agonize about how the features of every day are going to develop, what does that communicate about commitment to our Lord? Jesus taught His disciples: *"You're blessed when you're at the end of your rope. With less of you there is more of God and his rule'"* *(Matthew 5:3, The Msg.)*. Why do we habitually wait until we are overcome with desperation before we call on God?

"Worry is an old man with bended head, carrying a load of feathers which he thinks are lead" (Corrie ten Boom). Worry has a way of confusing or disorienting our thoughts. When we allocate our time to fretting about circumstances over which we have no control, we waste precious moments that could be spent in prayer, drawing us closer to God and the gift of perfect peace with which He lovingly desires to overwhelm us.

The Apostle Paul understood the human tendency to spiral downward as we focus on anxiety during stress, grief, or emergencies. He advised, *"Don't fret or worry. Instead of worrying, pray. Let petitions and praises shape your worries into prayers, letting God know your concerns. Before you know it, a sense of God's wholeness, everything coming together for good, will come and settle you down. It's wonderful what happens when Christ displaces worry at the center of your life'"* *(Philippians 4:6-7, The Msg.)*. Paul urges us to concentrate on things with eternal value, and to release our worry through prayer, leading us into deeper spiritual territory, where God transforms us with encouragement and power.

Anxiety results from the incapacity to deal with disturbing details. If we are tempted to ruminate an issue, God provides the productive alternative: *"Cast all your anxiety on him* {the Lord}, *for he cares for you" (1 Peter 5:7).* The ideal solution involves admitting disobedience, asking forgiveness, and giving God preeminence in all areas of our lives. Jesus asks, *"'Can all your worries add a single moment to your life?'" (Matthew 6:27, NLT).*

Worry stalls the growth and development of our personal relationship with Jesus, who advises that we not fret about our daily needs. *"'These things dominate the thoughts of unbelievers, but your heavenly Father already knows all your needs. Seek the kingdom of God above all else, and live righteously, and he will give you everything you need'" (Mathew 6:32-33, NLT).* We have knowledge of the totality of God's promises in his Word. Like Abraham and Sarah, are we apprehensive about God's timetable, jumping ahead of His plans for our lives?

Jesus, the Prince of Peace, grants wholeness and well-being for those who trust Him absolutely. Believers experience tranquility of spirit when they commit their troubles to God in prayer and worry about them no more. With open hands we transfer our cares to Jesus. Then we immediately close our fists, preventing us from reclaiming the same troubles. Jesus disposes of our miserable care package of worry, supplanting harmony, serenity, and comfort. Christ is in the business of transforming insecure lives to the enduring stability of peace. Depend upon Jesus always and in all ways! Forsake fickle, frail frustrations for Jesus' promise of peace!

RED STAINED PURITY

A wedding gown represents the potential for beautiful memories, reflects a significant investment, and is absolutely dazzling in purity. Brides-to-be typically spend many hours shopping for a unique gown, the one dress they've dreamed about for years. Prior to the wedding, the bride protects her gown from prying eyes and from damage. Imagine the reactions of horror when red wine splashes on the flawless gown the afternoon before a candlelight ceremony. Red, indelible stains on pure white—a shocking contrast! There's no way to effectively remove dark stains from white satin and lace. The gown is ruined. Panic erupts throughout the wedding party. Every bride seeks perfection for her wedding day. Her gown of choice must be sacrificed until an appropriate substitute can be found a few hours before the ceremony.

When He was incarnated on earth, Jesus left His glory and throne in heaven, where He was one with His heavenly Father. Both of them participated in every aspect of creation. Jesus Christ, the Son of God, is the purest person who ever lived. He is God. He is radiant and resplendent; flawless and undefiled.

Wherever He journeyed on earth, Jesus lived the way He preached. Motives for His actions were holy. His heart was immaculate from lack of sin. As pure white as new-fallen snow, Jesus glistens as a pearl in an oyster shell; unblemished as a newborn baby's skin; brilliant as bolts of flashing lightning against an ebony sky. There is nothing on earth with which to compare Jesus' purity, for He is heaven-sent.

In the Old Testament, God's temple laws required specific unblemished animals to be sacrificed regularly. Spilled blood was God's requirement to atone for all sin. The animals had to be perfect, neither spotted in color nor physically defective. For centuries the covenant of sacrificing animals was performed by priests to redeem the peoples' sins. Though it wasn't the optimum system, it was God's approved method until the promised Messiah was sacrificed on earth as the atonement for man's sin, a permanent solution for the ages.

As long ago as 600 B. C., the prophet Isaiah foretold Jesus' sacrificial death, providing a figurative account of the consequence of forgiveness through the Messiah's shed blood. *"Though your sins are like scarlet, they shall be white as snow; though they are red as crimson, they shall be like wool" (Isaiah 1:18).* Forgiveness is conditioned upon belief in the Lord Jesus Christ, necessitating a change of heart and lifestyle to conform to our Savior's love.

Death by Roman crucifixion was agonizing and atrocious. No one has ever suffered on the cross as Jesus did. In addition to the horrific physical torture and pain, Jesus bore the sins of all people from the past, present, and future generations of the world. A perfect sacrifice for our sins, Jesus was pristine and pure. His life for ours, for people of all time; Jesus, the guiltless one for the guilty, the sinless one for the sinner. As Jesus bled and died, He did so that we may live a spiritually victorious life. Three days later Jesus arose from the grave, conquering sin forever.

The Roman officers dishonored our Lord's innocence by striking Him and spitting in His face, verbally taunting Him, pulling his beard, and grinding a wreathe of thorns down over His forehead. His back was flogged, shredding the skin that was pressed against the roughly hewn timber of the cross. By the time Jesus reached the top of Golgotha Hill, He could barely walk. His body was exhausted, dehydrated, bleeding, and mangled.

Sin, faithless rebellion against God's laws, may seem inconsequential to man, but God abhors defiant thoughts, words, or actions by the creature against the authority of the Creator, establishing a deep chasm between God and man. Jesus offered His perfectly sinless body as the sacrifice required by the justice of God to save humanity from sin. Our Savior's blood gushed from His wounds, staining an undefiled life, bridging the gap between mankind and a holy God. Jesus acquired our burden of guilt, saturating His physically tormented body with His holy lifeblood.

Jesus' glory will never fade. His power will never diminish. But His love will grow ever more endearing. Jesus commanded us, *"'Store up for yourselves treasures in heaven... For where your treasure is, there your heart will be also'" (Matthew 6:20-21).* Jesus admonishes us to consider our priorities on earth in view of our future eternal life.

Similar to wedding vows, Jesus personifies purity, a major investment for the future, and a decision that will change the course of a person's life. There the similarities end. Christ is our living Savior, Lord, and King, who loves us, died, and rose again to redeem our sins, providing the only means to secure life eternal in heaven. What is your individual response to such a love-saturated, free gift that entitles each believer to fellowship with our Savior in heaven forevermore?

Some brides pay an exorbitant price for their perfect wedding gown. However, one drop of our Savior's blood is more valuable than the most exquisite gown intricately embellished with glittering diamonds.

JOY'S GRANDEUR

On a second missionary journey, Paul and Silas traveled to Philippi, a leading city where Roman customs were observed and idols worshipped. There the two missionaries were repeatedly confronted by a demon-possessed slave girl who made her owners wealthy by fortune-telling. *"Finally Paul became so annoyed that he turned around and said to the spirit, 'In the name of Jesus Christ I command you to come out of her!' At that moment the spirit left her"* (Acts 16:18). Realizing their lucrative business had evaporated right before their eyes, the girl's owners seized Paul and Silas, dragged them into the public square before the city magistrates, and claimed false charges against them. As mob involvement grew to a feverish pitch, the men were stripped, beaten, and thrown into jail.

The missionaries were flogged, a severe form of beating bare skin. The Romans used a whip fashioned of several leather straps with lead or bone embedded at the ends, which tore open wide, deep gashes of skin. By law, Jews restricted the number of lashes to thirty-nine, but the Romans had no limitations. Victims of Roman flogging often didn't survive the savage punishment.

Following their beating, the two men were led into an inner prison cell where their feet were fixed in stocks to serve as torture and added security. Physically their bodies were beaten and bloody, but their jubilant spirits could not be subdued. Their hearts rejoiced. Paul and Silas knew that all power, joy, and victory reside in Christ alone. They were confident they were serving a faithful God who would intervene on their behalf. *"About midnight Paul and Silas were praying and singing hymns to God, and the other prisoners were listening to them. Suddenly there was such a violent earthquake that the foundations of the prison were shaken. At once all the prison doors flew open, and everyone's chains came loose" (Acts 16:25-26).* Vision and trust beyond their current plight induced the missionaries' spontaneous, resounding praises to God.

The two men's witness in song communicated far more to the other prisoners than any sermons they could have preached. *"My lips will shout for joy when I will sing praise to you—I whom you have delivered. My tongue will tell of your righteous acts" (Psalm 71:23).* If joy were dependent on circumstances, Paul and Silas would have cowered due to pain and injustice. But they were assured that God's protection was sufficient. In similar circumstances, how many of us detect songs of praise spontaneously erupting from hearts saturated with joy?

Joy is dynamic, exuberant, and contagious, a constant dimension of a life of faith. Joy flows freely from dwelling in the Lord's presence. Not humanly manufactured, joy is endowed by God, urging us to praise Him in all circumstances. Cultivating a life of delightful rejoicing demonstrates a close relationship with God, for He is the source, the benevolent provider of all exultation. In God's Word, joy is a command; *"Rejoice always in the Lord" (Philippians 4:4),* and a gift *(Galatians 5:22),* confirming that when God assigns a task to His children, He lavishes them with enthusiasm to finish His work.

Any receptacle that overflows quickly spreads its contents into surrounding areas, seeping into cracks, permanently staining, leaking into remote spots to be discovered at a later time. Similarly, Jesus' attribute of joy is incapable of containment. It multiplies in the lives of believers, who carry it throughout the world.

A dam of negativity is unable to restrain our grateful hearts. Joy rolls along like a somersaulting snowball, picking up peace, trust, and hope, wrapping them into a spectacular bundle of unmitigated worship. Trudging through uphill trails of adversity, layers of zeal, strength, and courage naturally melt, seeping into the pathways of life, leaving behind evidence of an intimate relationship with our Savior. Dispersing love ministers to others, harvested by those who are desperate to experience eternal peace and comfort.

Jesus provides inside-out rejoicing, filling our hearts with a deluge of effervescence. *"You turned my wailing into dancing; you removed my sackcloth and clothed me with joy, that my heart may sing praises and not be silent. Lord my God, I will praise you forever"* *(Psalm 30:11-12).* Sackcloth, a symbol of mourning, is replaced by songs of exuberant praise. From the riches of heaven's own wardrobe room, swishing, elegant robes of rejoicing define us externally as the light of Christ's joy engulfs our hearts, offering supernatural encouragement. Jesus said, *"'If you keep my commands, you will remain in my love, just as I have kept my Father's commands and remain in his love. I have told you this so that my joy may be in you and that your joy may be complete'" (John 15:10-11).*

Joy has the potential to leap boundaries. Those who know Jesus personally acknowledge the splendor of His majesty, initiating a reaction that can best be described as dynamic, triumphant joy forevermore. *"My heart leaps for joy, and with my song I praise him" (Psalm 28:7b).* When was the last time you spiritually leaped for joy, demonstrating the thrill of victory with eternal consequences?

When Paul and Silas rejoiced in prayer and song, they weren't aware of the exceeding great plan God had devised. *"The jailer brought them into his house and set a meal before them; he was filled with joy because he had come to believe in God—he and his whole household" (Acts 16:34).*

Joy is the consistent result of trusting Jesus. Joy divided is multiplied. "To get the full value of joy, you must have someone to divide it with" (Mark Twain). Joy is contagious. Let us be zealous carriers, proliferating joy's impact throughout the world.

TAUNTS AND TRIUMPH

When he visited his three older brothers at the battlefield to deliver food, David didn't anticipate he would gain insight into military tactics, heighten the conflict, and earn status as a national hero.

Israel was at war with the Philistines, their perpetual enemy. It was the Philistine's policy to conserve warriors by deciding issues of war through a champion. One soldier from each camp typically met in combat in the valley between opposing armies sequestered on hilltops. Adopted from the ancient Greeks, the Philistine tactic struck rigid terror in the hearts of the Israeli troops. Unprepared, the Israelites were caught at a definite disadvantage. They had no physical giants in their fighting force and fewer men with a colossal amount of courage. Thus, a stand-off ensued.

Goliath, the Philistine giant, stood nine feet, nine inches tall. He was protected by layers of impenetrable iron armor everywhere but his face. David heard Goliath bleat his usual chants of defiance to Israel. Twice daily for forty days, Goliath delivered his challenging taunts: *"'Choose one man to come down here and fight me! If he kills me, then we will be your slaves. But if I kill him, you will be our slaves! I defy the armies of Israel today! Send me a man who will fight me!'" (1 Samuel 17:8b-10, NLT).*

Forty days is a long interval to contemplate a formidable foe without taking action, time for the Israeli soldiers to acquire an overload of accumulated pessimism. The troops and King Saul were demoralized and terrorized. Fear devastated their faith and trust in God. The fighting men were searching for security and relief from a human source. God's sovereign promise of support was scorned by the Israeli soldiers, who believed that Goliath, rather than their own God, was invincible.

The army's paralyzing fear demonstrated that they had lost all recollection of God's covenant promise to destroy their enemies in the Promised Land. Victory was conditional, contingent on the people trusting and obeying their Lord. *"When you prepare for battle, the priest must come forward to speak to the troops. He will say to them, 'Listen to me, all of you men of Israel! Do not be afraid as you go out to fight your enemies today! Do not lose heart or panic or tremble before them. For the Lord is going with you! He will fight for you against your enemies, and he will give you victory'" (Deuteronomy 20:2-4, NLT).* Curiously, neither king nor priest reminded the militia of God's rich covenant promise, as they were commanded.

David, at age sixteen, had recently been anointed the next king of Israel, the shepherd of God's people, and he was planning to defend the threatened and frightened flock. Although there were financial rewards and other perks for the victor who killed the Philistine giant, David was especially grieved that God's honor had been violated by Goliath's accusations. *"'This pagan Philistine ... has defied the armies of the living God. The Lord who rescued me {David} from the claws of the lion and the bear will rescue me from the hand of this Philistine!'" (1 Samuel 17:36b-37, NLT).*

When David heard Goliath's threats, he volunteered to fight the giant. Immediately scoffers dismissed him. King Saul personally attempted to discourage him by reminding David he was only a boy facing a professionally trained, career warrior. Goliath sneered in contempt and cursed David, calling him a dog.

David was unable to instantly fabricate courage at such a critical juncture. He lived a life of constant obedience, depending on God's provisions and faithfulness. When an emergency situation arose, David recognized his source of power, assured he could lean heavily on God. By slaying Goliath, David exhibited heroic faith, empowered exclusively by God's sovereign strength and accuracy.

Courage is not the absence of fear, but the commitment to perform in the midst of fear. Every day we are confronted with intimidating situations. Do we seek God's guidance in prayer as our first response? His promises to us are just as valid as they were to the Israelite nation centuries ago. *"'Have I not commanded you? Be strong and courageous. Do not be afraid; do not be discouraged, for the Lord, your God will be with you wherever you go'" (Joshua 1:9).* God is bigger and more powerful than any of our foes, no matter how insurmountable they may appear.

Like us, David possessed fear, a normal human reaction to threats or danger. God desires to relieve us of the emotional stress created by intimidating situations: fear of criticism, panic of public speaking, dread of death; even our personal insecurities are masked fears. King David wrote, *"'I sought the Lord, and he answered me; he delivered me from all my fears'"* (Psalm 34:4).

Do our lives demonstrate consistent trust and obedience? Asking God to intervene is commonly relegated as a last resort. That need not be, according to our Lord's assurances. *"'Never will I leave you; never will I forsake you.' So we say with confidence, 'the Lord is my helper; I will not be afraid. What can mere mortals do to me?'"* (Hebrews 13:5-6).

The next time your heart freezes with fear, whisper a quick prayer to Jesus. In a time-sensitive situation, simply cry, "Help!" When we experience shock, words often elude us, but we are assured that God knows our predicament; He has made provisions for every scenario. As believers, our spirits are joined with the Spirit of God. During those times when fear renders us spiritually mute, *"The Holy Spirit prays for us with groanings that cannot be expressed in words. And the Father who knows all hearts knows what the Spirit is saying, for the Spirit pleads for us believers in harmony with God's own will"* (Romans 8:26b-27, NLT).

How many giants do we face who threaten to reduce us to a quivering mass of ineffectual fear? God's directions remain the same as centuries ago. *"'Do not be afraid or discouraged … for the battle is not yours, but God's. Stand firm and see the deliverance the Lord will give you'"* (2 Chronicles 20:15b, 17b). Our Lord will slay giants so monumental we cannot see past them, for God is our ultimate source of power and victory. We may face situations beyond our reserves, but never beyond God's resources.

GREAT EXPECTATIONS

G azing at the bleak winter landscape, one observes a definite lack of color, a bland outlook with no life stirring. With barren expectancy, we prepare our hearts for desolation, reflected in attitudes and conversation. Comparing heart focus with environmental conditions is risky, thwarting inward hope and personal growth. Though it is easy to be affected by the lack of sunshine and warmth in winter, let us not permit exterior influences to eclipse heart radiance with which Jesus penetrates darkness by reflecting His light throughout our lives. Joy is quickly extinguished by despondency.

"Now faith is confidence in what we hope for and assurance about what we do not see" (Hebrews 11:1). After Jesus' disciple, Thomas, conquered his disbelief at Christ's post-resurrection appearance, Jesus taught His disciples, *"'Because you have seen me, you have believed; blessed are those who have not seen and yet have believed'" (John 20:29).* Faith, the consequence of trust, is securely locked within our hearts. Trust is the outgrowth of belief.

Focusing on the negative, our hearts languish with despair. The pessimistic approach embodied by a curmudgeon is so discouraging that black clouds spontaneously open, dispensing chilly water on new ideas. Cynics have an intimidating influence on positive thoughts, much like the austere environment in winter.

With whom do we communicate to enliven a joyful spirit? God is the author and creator of all things good. *"Jesus answered, 'No one is good—except God alone'" (Mark 10:18).* The goodness God constantly imparts to us is a reflection of His divine character of purity and holiness.

After contemplating the monotonous winter panorama once again, rather than the revision of scenery, one discovers the need for an attitude adjustment. God has the ability to alter our perspective with His gifts of joy and peace. Man is unable to contrive sovereign gifts independently with the power of positive thinking, as some assert. We must rely on our Lord to supply us with His limitless attributes, always available to those who seek Him. *"Take on an entirely new way of life—a God-fashioned life, a life renewed from the inside and working itself into your conduct as God accurately reproduces his character in you" (Ephesians 4:24, The Msg.).* We are commanded to fellowship with God, the glorious, victorious Creator of life and light, peace and joy, love and grace; revising our lives forever by placing them in God's care. *"Submit yourself, then, to God ... Come near to God and he will come near to you" (James 4:7-8).* God never changes, but His followers tend to waver in and out of fellowship with Him. Our Lord calls us back to a consistent, intimate relationship.

Winter, with its unique season of dormancy and hibernation, is also a period of refreshment, preparing for regrowth, for a magnificent burst of beauty and fragrance that identifies the imminent season of spring. Let us not bear winter grudgingly, but joyfully use the time to develop attitudes pleasing to God. There is beauty during winter unseen at other times of the year. Shadows on snow peek around trees, marching like toy soldiers as the sun manipulates imaginary forms. Sunsets of majestic proportions and beauty light up late afternoon skies with unequivocal displays of prismatic colors. The deep green of softwood trees and the silhouettes of stark hardwoods in the foreground of high, pristine snowbanks create fantastic visual delights. A full moon illuminates light blue blankets of snow when the dark draperies of night are pulled down upon the world.

What do you envision in the winter season of your life? The bleakness of financial, health, or employment woes, or the unprecedented power, protection, and provisions offered by God Himself? Seek the attitude that reflects Jesus' submission and obedience to His Father just prior to His crucifixion. *"'Abba, Father,' he cried out, 'everything is possible for you. Please take this cup of suffering away from me. Yet I want your will to be done, not mine'"* (Mark 14:36, NLT).

Jesus could release His deepest hope to His heavenly Father, assured that even at such a late hour God could perform the impossible by cancelling His Son's crucifixion. Yet, Jesus trusted His Father's perfect plan, convinced that His hope wasn't misplaced by cross-your-fingers wishful thinking, but as confident expectations resting on God's promises, free of worry and nail biting. Jesus trusted in God's sovereign ability to answer His prayer custom-designed for His Son alone. He invites us to do the same.

Hope is like a ship's anchor securely snagged at the bottom of the sea. The Christian anchor rises up into the heavenly realms, guaranteeing personal security. *"We have this hope as an anchor for the soul, firm and secure" (Hebrews 6:19).* It is essential for us to value God above all else in our lives, for He freely extends anchoring hope, joyful delight, and unmerited grace.

Ask God to transform your priorities. He will lavish you abundantly with the righteousness of Jesus. To live right before God (righteousness) is His ultimate goal for each believer. *"The Lord delights in those who fear him, who put their hope in his unfailing love" (Psalm 147:11).* Believers who relinquish their worries to God and dwell on them no more, experience inner tranquility. Then the victory of God is theirs to enjoy.

"And the peace of God, which transcends all understanding, will guard your hearts and your minds in Christ Jesus" (Philippians 4:7). The full dimension of God's love and provisions are beyond our comprehension, motivating us to trust Him explicitly.

Just as the exterior world perpetually changes, believers also experience dependable growth and renewal as their spiritual relationship with God expands. We learn patience and perseverance, but most marvelous of all is the imperceptible growth in hope, trust, and faith our Lord accomplishes by His power at work within us, transforming our lives. Expect the unexpected from an exceptional, extraordinary God!

EXCUSES, EXCUSES...

G od called Moses to lead His people to freedom, terminating four hundred years of slavery. As God's representative, Moses would stipulate non-negotiable terms of release with the Egyptian Pharaoh. Moses resisted his assignment with repeated, feeble excuses, pleading with God, *"'Please send someone else'"* *(Exodus 4:13)*. God had already chosen an assistant and said to Moses, *"'What about your brother, Aaron the Levite ... He is already on his way to meet you ... You shall speak to him and put words in his mouth; I will help both of you speak and will teach you what to do'"* *(vv. 14b-15)*. After declining a fifth and final time, Moses finally accepted God's commission. To allay his fears, God demonstrated miracles Moses could perform when facing Pharaoh.

Moses' stubborn resistance collapsed in submission to God's authority and divine assistance. His stalwart determination, obedience, and allegiance to God and his people strengthened with each future adversity blocking his path, providing a pattern for all Christians to follow. Moses learned the roles of advocate and intercessor for the Israelites, pleading with God several times to save the nation when God was so angry with their rebellion He was prepared to annihilate the entire population, dubbing them a stiff-necked people.

Though initially manifesting anxiety that exposed a faltering faith, Moses later achieved monumental triumphs in his career as an extraordinary leader, lawgiver, and spokesman for Israel. Not a natural-born leader, Moses gradually learned to shepherd his people during a lifetime of service.

How do we respond when God presents us with an assignment that we hesitate to perform? Like Moses, are we primarily worried about our personal frailty and faults? Christians are adept at devising clever excuses when God requires that we step outside our comfort zones. Lack of faith is usually responsible for blocking our paths of obedience.

God focuses on our availabilities rather than our abilities. He uses common people for uncommon jobs. And, He always walks before us, preparing our paths, leading us with His mighty power. "God has never sent any difficulties into the lives of His children without His accompanying offer of help in this life and reward in the life to come" (Billy Graham).

God hasn't changed during the centuries since Moses lived, still promising strength and leadership with every mission He assigns. The Apostle Paul said, "'I can do all things through him who gives me strength'" (Philippians 4:13). If we believe in God's Word, we receive power to accomplish God's work.

Imagine the pleasure of strolling the paths of a flower garden, inhaling the sweet fragrance naturally emitted from mature blossoms. *"Now he {God} uses us to spread the knowledge of Christ everywhere, like a sweet perfume. Our lives are a Christ-like fragrance rising up to God" (2 Corinthians 2:14b-15, NLT).* When we accept Christ as our Lord and Savior, we are transformed by His grace. Then, even in the midst of suffering, we emit the sweet fragrance of love that wafts up to God and radiates out to others.

Our lives are letters written by the Holy Spirit for all to read. The apostle Paul explained to fellow Christians: *"'You yourselves are our letter, written on our hearts, known and read by everyone. You show that you are a letter from Christ, the result of our ministry, written not with ink but with the Spirit of the living God, not on tablets of stone but on tablets of human hearts'" (2 Corinthians 3:2-3).* Is your life a letter that captivates readers' interest, from which they acquire great truth and knowledge of Jesus? Our lives are the only Bible some people will ever read. May your relationship with God be a life permeated with dependency and obedience that will brighten and fragrance paths for others to follow. Reflect on a poetic explanation:

"The Gospel is written a chapter a day
By deeds that you do and by words that you say.
Men read what you say, whether faithless or true.
Say, what is the Gospel according to you?" (Anon)

Jesus said, *"'You are the salt of the earth. But what good is salt if it has lost its flavor? You are the light of the world—like a city on a hilltop that cannot be hidden. In the same way, let your good deeds shine out for all to see, so that everyone will praise your heavenly*

Father'" (Matthew 5:13a, 14, 16, NLT). A Christian's primary function is to glorify God. Spiritual effectiveness is determined by our ability to flavor and light the world for Christ. God-centered lives honor our Father in heaven, witness to His goodness, and proclaim His salvation. Believers possess no inherent light; Christ shines His light through them, penetrating a dark world.

Jesus told his disciples, *"'Go and make disciples of all the nations, baptizing them in the name of the Father and the Son and the Holy Spirit. Teach these new disciples to obey all the commands I have given you. And be sure of this: I am with you always, even to the end of the age'"* (Matthew 28:19-20, NLT). The risen Savior commanded His Word be preached to all people, in every nation. Though few of us will serve as missionaries in a foreign land, each believer is a disciple of Christ. The old adage, "bloom where you are planted," indicates the most effective place to communicate Jesus' message of salvation is within our own circles of influence.

When God requests that we embark on a new spiritual challenge, it is wise for us to avoid Moses' initial reactions. Making excuses to avoid serving is contradictory to our claims as followers of Christ. It is futile to argue with God. In doing so, we minimize our participation in miraculous victories. God has demonstrated His faithfulness and trustworthiness throughout the ages. Now we have the opportunity to serve Him enthusiastically and wholeheartedly, as He empowers us to accomplish the work He assigns. "Experience is the hardest teacher because it gives a test first and the lessons afterward" (Lindsay Thomas).

MORTAL MEETS IMMORTAL

E nvision that you were standing in the very presence of Jesus when He walked this earth, so close you could reach out to touch Christ as He healed all manner of illness and disability. Most diseases in Jesus' day had no cure. Imagine celebrating exuberantly with those individuals who, within seconds, were transformed from a life of physical or mental misery into complete health. Those who formerly depended on others to provide their most basic bodily needs, were suddenly converted to wellness and independent living by mere words from Jesus.

A desperate woman who had suffered a hemorrhagic affliction for twelve years, had exhausted her finances consulting numerous physicians, with no relief for her effort. Her life was limited; constant bleeding isolated her and rendered her unclean, preventing her from worshiping in the temple. She had heard that the Healer was in town, so she devised a plan. Her most critical aspiration was jostling through the tightly congested crowd pressing against Jesus. She was convinced that a slight touch of His flowing outer cloak would sufficiently transfer Jesus' healing powers to her ravaged body. Whether the diseased woman's scheme was premeditated or if she acted on impulse, we will never know. Of one fact we can be sure—she needed her plan to succeed.

"'Who touched me?' Jesus asked." (Luke 8:45a).

Being exposed wasn't part of the woman's plan. She comingled with the crowd engulfing Jesus, intending to quickly touch Jesus' clothing, then discreetly slip away healed and unnoticed. It wasn't Jesus' method to perform healings on demand without personal interaction. He came to earth as the Son of God to accomplish the will of His Father in heaven, to obey Him explicitly, and to bring glory to His name. Jesus wouldn't permit the woman to recede into the crowd before He announced her healing and she made a public profession of faith.

"Jesus said, 'Someone touched me. I know that power has gone out from me'" (Luke 8:46). With crowds of people encircling Jesus, it was inevitable that several in the group casually brushed His clothing or unintentionally bumped against Him. Jesus knew the one who contacted Him hadn't brushed His clothing accidentally. The woman's touch was different and distinct; light but intentional. She probably stretched her arm to its maximum length from as far away as possible, believing that a delicate touch of Jesus' garment would transmit healing power to her body.

When Jesus inquired about the person in the crowd who had touched Him, the disciples were indifferent. Peter addressed the peculiar question for all of them. *"'Master, the people are crowding and pressing against you'" (Luke 8:45b).* The disciples thought it futile to seek one elusive person among a massive crowd of admirers, but Jesus never ignores those who sincerely search for Him.

"Then the woman, seeing that she could not go unnoticed, came trembling and fell at his feet. In the presence of all the people, she told why she had touched him and how she had been instantly healed" (Luke 8:47). Mortals cannot interact with the immortal without phenomenal results occurring. A person is always empowered or energized; changes occur like fireworks illuminating a pitch black sky. Jesus didn't touch the woman; she reached out to touch Him, resulting in instant healing. *"Then he said to her, 'Daughter, your faith has healed you. Go in peace.'" (v. 48).* In the Gospel account, this woman is the only individual Jesus addressed as daughter, a tender term Jesus used to express compassion for her suffering and praise for her faith.

When we approach Jesus in prayer, is it with a believing heart overflowing with trust? Or do we, like some in the crowd, doubt a brush with Jesus will have lasting consequences? We are commanded to manifest a solid belief in Jesus, reflecting faith, convinced that He has an ultimate purpose for our individual lives. *"Confident of this, that he who began a good work in you will carry it on to completion until the day of Christ Jesus." (Philippians 1:6).*

The woman touched Jesus with intent, convinced that when she boldly reached out to Him, Jesus would respond with healing powers. Jesus never disappoints! Let us react in prayer like the suffering woman Jesus commended for her faith, unlike the crowds of complacent curiosity seekers who knew not the depth of love and power in their midst.

"For the Spirit God gave us does not make us timid, but gives us power, love and self-discipline" (2 Timothy 1:7). Though we do not physically stand in the presence of Jesus today, He is ever-present in our lives, encouraging us to commune with him through prayer. Like the woman who was determined to touch Jesus' garment, our outreach may be vague, even tentative, but with boldness and confidence we are privileged to call on Almighty God, knowing He answers each of our prayers. Jesus is just as accessible to us in prayer spiritually as His physical presence was attainable to the suffering woman. She approached Jesus with confidence and courage, the methods with which we are commanded to pray. The difference is that the woman walked toward Jesus physically trembling in fear. We are to seek Him reverently and submit to His will, unafraid of His presence and power.

Jesus is equally as available to us as He was to the people who solicited His attention centuries ago. We need not push through crowds to reach Him. Our faint call to Jesus alerts Him to our troubles immediately, assuring us of His undivided attention. Our Lord then responds from His throne in heaven and His residence in our hearts, adjusting responses to conform to His sovereign plans for our individual lives.

COMPLIMENTED BY SHEEP

In the ancient Near East, the Israelites were nomadic herdsmen; plains were dotted with sheep. The nation of Israel was dependent on sheep for its livelihood: wool for coats, leather for tents, milk and meat for sustenance, and live animals for temple sacrifices and offerings. Both Jacob and Job were wealthy patriarchs, their prosperity determined by the size of their livestock herds. Jacob was *"exceedingly prosperous and came to own large flocks {of sheep} ... and camels and donkeys" (Genesis 30:43)*. Job *"owned seven thousand sheep, three thousand camels, five hundred yoke of oxen and five hundred donkeys." (Job 1:3)*

Sheep are mentioned in the Bible more frequently than any other animal. It seems natural, then, that many narratives and parables in God's Word use illustrations of shepherds and sheep. Kings in Old Testament times were often referred to as shepherd-leaders of their people. Jesus said, *"'I am the good shepherd; I know my sheep and my sheep know me—just as the Father knows me and I know the Father—and I lay down my life for the sheep'" (John 10:14-15)*. How miraculous that Jesus describes our shepherd-sheep relationship with Him in terms He shares with His heavenly Father!

Jesus' role extends beyond that of our shepherd to that of our Shepherd-King. He is our salvation, security, and strength. We recognize His voice and respond with obedience. *"Know that the Lord is God ... We are his people, the sheep of his pasture" (Psalm 100:3).* The shepherd invests his life caring for his flock. Such timid, docile animals are content to remain in the presence of their shepherd as Christians thrive in the nearness of their Lord.

The New Testament church was compared to a sheepfold and Jesus to the shepherd who protected the gate of the fold. The sheepfold is an enclosure where sheep gather in a flock at night. The shepherd sleeps at the entrance—the door or the gate of the fold—positioning his body between the defenseless sheep and nocturnal predators, scavengers, or thieves. Jesus is our door. Nothing threatens us without first alerting Him to danger. He is a living gate of the sheepfold, protecting us, His sheep. Jesus said, *"'I am the gate; whoever enters through me will be saved. They will come in and go out, and find pasture'" (John 10:9).* In Jesus there is safety. We have freedom to rest and have all of our needs supplied by the Great Shepherd, our Lord and Savior.

Israeli shepherds led their sheep rather than driving them. Sheep responded exclusively to their shepherd's voice and the shepherd knew each animal in his flock. *"He calls his own sheep by name and leads them out ... He goes on ahead of them, and his sheep follow him because they know his voice. But they will never follow a stranger; in fact, they will run away from him because they do not recognize a stranger's voice" (John 10:3b-5).*

Sheep are dumb, but curious animals. A sheep that wanders from the sheepfold is unable to find its way back. The shepherd must keep a keen eye on each member of the flock. Frequently an animal that roams gets entangled in briers, helpless to move. It may get mired in a water hole, or it may stumble over a cliff, lying injured below. The shepherd leaves the flock to search for one lost lamb. When he locates it, he tenderly wraps the frightened lamb in his coat and carries it to safety on his shoulders. Our Shepherd-Lord rescues us in a similar manner. *"Let the beloved of the Lord rest secure in him, for he shields him all day long, and the one the Lord loves rests between his shoulders" (Deuteronomy 33:12)*, the place of safety.

Sheep are social animals and prefer to live in a flock for safety and warmth. If one animal meanders from the fold without a shepherd to follow, the lamb's sense of direction is confused and it is quickly lost. As long as the shepherd is within hearing distance, sheep will bed down, comfortable and protected. Our Great Shepherd offers protection, and provision for us. *"'I myself will tend my sheep and have them lie down,' declares the Sovereign Lord. 'I will search for the lost and bring back the strays. I will bind up the injured and strengthen the weak'" (Ezekiel 34:15-16a)*.

We are created with free wills, but we frequently neglect to use our intelligence wisely, making poor choices, creating consequences reacting like a wandering, lost lamb. Jesus, our Shepherd-King, promises to lead, to strengthen, and to rescue us from danger. He sacrificed His own life to redeem the spiritually lost. Those who know Jesus respond to His voice and to His leadership. *"'My sheep listen to my voice; I know them, and they follow me. I give them eternal life, and they will never perish. No one can snatch them away from me, for my Father has given them to me, and he is more powerful than anyone else. No one can snatch them from the Father's hand. The Father and I are one'" (John 10:27-30, NLT).*

Sheep and their shepherds symbolize the relationship the Great Shepherd desires with believers. Sheep are ideal models of submission: followers, not leaders; obedient to one shepherd; reacting to his call; comfortable in his presence. They rely on their shepherd for food, protection, and treatment of injuries. Jesus admonishes us to follow Him with similar dependency and trust.

Being compared to sheep may offend human pride, but Jesus himself designed the appropriate analogy. Like lambs, do we follow our Great Shepherd as if our lives depend upon His leadership? Let us humbly recall the numerous occasions when our Shepherd-Lord rescued us from prickly brier patches of temptation and thorny thickets of sin. *"For you were like sheep going astray, but now you have returned to the Shepherd and Overseer of your souls" (1 Peter 2:25).* Perhaps being compared to sheep is a spiritual compliment after all!

TENSION OR TRUST

T he moments are tense, the anxiety palpable. The body language of the sweat-beaded brow, darting eyes, and twitching lips speaks volumes. A frightened person is easily recognizable. We have all experienced something so terrifying that it creates lasting emotional trauma. It is likely we can recite exact details from the encounter. Do we remember the fright or do we recall the overwhelming peace when we trusted God to intercede and deliver us?

The glory of God appeared to Abraham. *"'Leave your country and your people,' God said, 'and go to the land I will show you'"* (Acts 7:3). God commanded Abraham to leave the advanced civilization of Ur of the Chaldeans to travel to an unknown land for an unspecified period of time. Abraham obeyed without questioning. He trusted that God had an important reason for calling him out of his homeland and removing him from all things familiar. God's plan was to establish a people who acknowledged Him as their one true God in their new homeland, which He had promised Moses long before.

In the foreign lands where God led Abraham, he and his wife, Sarah, concocted a pact claiming to be siblings rather than marriage partners. The man who unquestionably obeyed His Lord, fabricated the story that Sarah was his sister, fearing he would be killed in ungodly territory for access to his naturally beautiful wife. Twice Abraham and Sarah engaged in a similar deception and twice the pharaoh of the land felt free to take Sarah for his wife. Twice their fear produced a lie.

Though they were disobedient, God didn't abandon His children. Each time one of the pharaohs prepared to marry Sarah, God inflicted such destruction on the king and the inhabitants of the land, Abraham and Sarah's plan was revealed. The irate pharaohs were eager to get rid of the two deceitful people whose God had imposed incredible harm. Apparently even the heathen cultures had morals; it was strictly forbidden to take another man's wife.

Abraham, the father of all nations and patriarch of the Old Testament, had a major confrontation with fear. We do not understand the reasons that motivated Sarah and Abraham to lie about their marriage; they had obviously trusted God in all other areas. When one of the pharaohs questioned Abraham pertaining to his motives, he attempted to validate his behavior with sinful deception. Abraham conceded they shared the same father, but different mothers, so he felt justified in asking Sarah to introduce him as her brother. The truth was that Abraham feared for his life. Rather than trust God to protect them in the foreign lands where He led them, Abraham relied on self-sufficiency and cunning. Lies identify fear.

Abraham and Sarah were not so unlike us. We often implement trust as a last resort. When all else fails, we come to God in emotional disarray. Sometimes our confidence has been tainted by the negative experiences of trusting other people. When the pressure mounts, when we are at our greatest risk, we often revert to our own meager resources. God promises, *"Never will I leave you; never will I forsake you. So we say with confidence, the Lord is my helper; I will not be afraid. What can man do to me?'"* *(Hebrews 13:5-6).* When trouble threatens, is our preferred first line of defense running straight into the protective arms of our heavenly Father?

Preoccupied with fear, Abraham withdrew from God, relying on his own strength. What Abraham needed was the super, sovereign amount of power that only God provides. God knew His servant's needs and intervened to create destruction in the lands where the pharaohs were planning to marry Sarah. God could see trouble brewing, but Abraham's sight was blinded by confidence in his distorted story. In the volatile situation, God protected all involved: Sarah was shielded from exploitation, Abraham from his own devious actions and a life-altering mistake, and the pharaohs from breaking the law of the land. God is faithful, interceding to protect all of His children.

Abraham was a work in progress. He made mistakes. Like Abraham, we err and lack good judgment. We fear our own emotions when we should be trusting God. Fear taunts, causing doubt and indecision. We want to gain control, but fear proves us inept and inefficient, weak and wavering. Prolonged anxiety incapacitates.

As a toddler, our son planted his small bicycle over the center of a massive mud puddle, locking the training wheels onto the edges. Then, he pedaled with all of his boundless childhood energy. The bicycle remained stationary while our son happily spewed an enormous fountain of mud, slathering his entire body with dirty slime. Like our toddler bicyclist, we are so adept at panicking that we are ineffectually riveted in place. Apprehension splashes over us. When it finally occurs to us to call to God for help, we are drenched with the mud of frantic pedaling through our own incompetent schemes.

Were it not for the grace and mercy of God, we would all wallow in perpetual, prolific fears. Our Lord commands us to be strong and courageous, believing in Him as our Source of trust. When we commit our total welfare to God, we need never fear.

Like Abraham during his spiritually immature years, initially we may exhibit convenient, random trust in God. As we grow in dependency and submission to God's will, we generate natural confident responses when fear assails. Abraham's faith matured as God graciously rescued him from his own inadequate reactions to fear. If we could ask Abraham's advice today, no doubt he would remind us: *"Trust in the Lord with all your heart; do not depend on your own understanding. Seek his will in all you do, and he will show you which path to take" (Proverbs 3:5-6, NLT).* Fear paralyzes; trust conquers.

RADIANCE OF GLORY

F ollowing sunrise, when the soft glow of early morning light filters through the labyrinth of tree branches, the ambience of autumn's aroma and activity disseminates. Rustled by gentle breezes, the crisp, dead leaves spontaneously flutter to earth, composing a barely audible tap of percussive rhythm. *"The Mighty One, God, the Lord, speaks and summons the earth from the rising of the sun to where it sets ... Perfect in beauty, God shines forth"* *(Psalm 50:1-2).*

From close proximity I viewed the border of trees. Brilliant red totally encompassed the maple tree placed in the front line of duty, embraced on all sides with multi-chromatic hardwood trees, proliferating conspicuously sublime rainbow colors. In the immediate foreground, a filigreed, green cedar tree was superimposed on the deeply layered, adorned forest, producing slices of autumn pigment in profusion.

In the wide open spaces where hills meet the sky and valleys separate hills, there exists a seasonal panoramic view of the vivid color spectrum of autumn hues proclaimed across wide stretches of geography, affirming that our Creator specializes in spectacular beauty. The illustrious saturation of colorful hues, like a distant patchwork quilt, is a grandiose proclamation of God's power and glory. *"The mountains and hills will burst into song before you, and all the trees of the field will clap their hands" (Isaiah 55:12),* figurative language expressing that God's creation joins in effervescent praise to celebrate the splendor with which our Lord surrounds His people in the physical world He engineered and created.

Oh, how the Lord lavishes us with His exalted beauty! In the sunlight, God's sovereign palette accentuates a wide range of flame-colored autumn leaves. From a distant perspective, the leaves mingle with puffy white clouds, waltzing across blue sky. God introduces astounding highlights to our daylight hours, followed by twinkling galaxies of stars draped across a nighttime ebony background. *"Be exalted, O God, above the heavens; let your glory be over all the earth" (Psalm 57:5).*

God's visible glory is always described in terms of brightness. Because this world's allure authenticates our Creator's unique signature, all of earth is infused with His splendor. *"The land was radiant with his {God's} glory" (Ezekiel 43:2b).* There is neither time nor place where our Lord's presence is not manifest with His handiwork. Let us glorify His resplendence with our praise of thanksgiving during every season of life!

GOD OF OUR FATHERS

Our three-year-old grandson liked playing with his mini plastic workbench and tool set. One day he announced his plan to perform a tune-up on his mother using his toy drill and chunky screws. Typical of a toddler's short attention span, after a few minutes he declared, "There, 'yer all screwed up!" Evidently he found a few loose screws—another problem tackled and solved by toddler expertise! How matter-of-factly children follow wherever their imaginations transport them. As children grow, we react with delight at their curiosity and creativity, complimenting their parents for their intelligent, precocious offspring.

Our heavenly Father came from eternity past to create humanity for His glory. God is all-powerful, all-knowing, and present everywhere at once. He never makes mistakes and always keeps His promises. How often are we astonished by miraculous acts of God or by His breathtaking natural creations? Do we routinely express astonishment and gratitude to Almighty God for holding the universe in balance with the same mighty hand with which He reaches out to us in love, mercy, and grace? God never changes, nor does He fail. His unlimited power is extraordinary, surpassing all things visible and intangible. Compare our frequency of complimenting

God to the number of times we overflow with effervescence when a child lovingly flings his arms around us or engages in realistic play. Although Jesus loves the little children and commands us to pattern our faith after their simplistic trust, He demands foremost worship as Lord of our lives.

What spectacular, out-of-this-world love the Father showers on us, the same intentional love that sent His Son to earth to die, to cleanse our sins, and to secure eternal life for those who believe. *"May the Lord lead your hearts into a full understanding and expression of the love of God and the patient endurance that comes from Christ" (2 Thessalonians 3:5, NLT).* How deserving is our Lord of our boundless worship of His immeasurable, inexhaustible love and grace!

To release the Israelites from four centuries of enslavement, God sent Moses as His representative to negotiate with the Egyptian Pharaoh. Moses, reluctant and afraid of rejection, asked what name he should use to introduce God to the Israelites. *"God replied to Moses, 'I AM WHO I AM. Say this to the people of Israel: I AM has sent me to you ... Yahweh, the God of your ancestors—the God of Abraham, the God of Isaac, and the God of Jacob—has sent me to you. This is my eternal name, my name to remember for all generations'" (Exodus 3:14-15, NLT).* His identification as God of their ancestors was important, reminding both Moses and the Israelites that *Yahweh* was not a new god, but the sovereign Lord of the Hebrews in the past, as He would be forevermore.

By distinguishing Himself as **I AM,** God clarified His eloquent, timeless nature. **I AM** discloses His unchanging, uncreated, self-existing person. Only God is able to define Himself. His infallible Word is permeated with descriptions of His unprecedented characteristics. *Yahweh,* His important Old Testament name means to be actively present with His people. God's divine character is confirmed by wisdom, righteousness, holiness, and love. *"For the foolishness of God is wiser than human wisdom, and the weakness of God is stronger than human strength" (1 Corinthians 1:25).* He indicates when it is necessary to detour our personal path to conform to His will. God's wisdom promotes the best action in the best way at the best time for His best purpose.

Pharaoh defiantly refused Moses' request to release the Israelites from bondage. He possessed a self-imposed hardened heart toward Israel's God, an unyielding resistance to affirm His divinity. Pharaoh maintained stubborn determination to promote his own personal delusions of deity as he embarked on a defiant collision course with the one, supreme God. At the outset of each new plague, Pharaoh pleaded to have the scourge discontinued, promising to liberate the Israelites if God complied. When God mercifully terminated the plague, Pharaoh reneged on his promise to release God's people. *The Lord … "is patient with you, not wanting anyone to perish, but everyone to come to repentance" (2 Peter 3:9).* Pharaoh tried God's patience, demonstrating stubborn indifference in his heart. Ultimately, it took ten plagues, including the death of all first-born males, impacting Pharaoh's own son, to motivate him to obey God. There is never a justifiable reason to exhibit a superior, proud attitude of self-righteousness toward God. From peasant or king, God demands worship in splendor and holiness.

Jesus commands us to adopt the simplistic, straightforward faith of a child. When His disciples argued which of them would be greatest in the Kingdom of Heaven, Jesus invited a little child to sit in their midst. *"And He said: 'Truly I tell you, unless you change and become like little children, you will never enter the kingdom of heaven. Therefore, whoever takes the lowly position of this child is the greatest in the kingdom of heaven. And whoever welcomes one such child in my name welcomes me'"* (Matthew 18:3-5). Whoever claims to be a child of God listens to Jesus and willingly obeys Him.

God sent His only Son to earth to redeem our sins. No matter how egregious the accusations against Jesus, no group of people or government possessed the power to crucify Jesus had it not been God's will. Jesus said, *"'For unless you believe that I AM who I claim to be, you will die in your sins. When you have lifted up the Son of Man on the cross, then you will understand that I AM he. I do nothing on my own but say what the Father taught me. And the one who has sent me is with me—he has not deserted me. For I always do what pleases him'"* (John 8:24b; 28-29, NLT).

Believers are known as simplehearted (Psalm 116:6), those who act childlike in their acceptance and trust of the Lord; super conquerors (Romans 8:27), who claim unsurpassed victory in Jesus. Christ often turns the world's priorities upside-down, demonstrating His sovereign justice. God hardened Pharaoh's heart, exposing his hypocrisy that led to his destruction, but He magnifies the simplistic faith of little children. Jesus' divine imperative directs us to revere, worship, and glorify Him with humble hearts, for our Lord is the great **I AM!**

FAITHFUL,
FABULOUS PROMISES

O n Resurrection Sunday, Jesus approached two men walking from Jerusalem to the village of Emmaus. When He joined the duo, they were raptly engrossed in conversation, with sad countenances. As Jesus walked beside Cleopas and his friend, neither recognized their Master's resurrection body.

The two disciples were amazed that the stranger hadn't heard the news about the events in Jerusalem during the past few days. Such a verbal exchange of current events would be comparable in our day to interrupting a conversation between people excitedly discussing the first moon landing, while the entire world was abuzz with the chatter. Surrounding Jerusalem over two thousand years ago, all conversation focused on the sensational news of the Jewish religious leaders handing Jesus over to be sentenced to death. They crucified Him King of the Jews and buried Him in a borrowed tomb.

Cleopas characterized his Master to the stranger. *"'He was a prophet powerful in word and deed before God and all the people, but we had hoped that he was the one who was going to redeem Israel'"* (Luke 24:19, 21). It is likely Cleopas meant the Israelites were hopeful Jesus would mount a military coup to defeat the Romans, and establish an independent Jewish nation. Now it seemed all hope was dashed.

Cleopas also lamented that women who were at the garden tomb early that morning found Jesus' tomb empty, with the large stone at the entrance rolled away. Angels at the tomb reported their Master was alive. Though other disciples confirmed the women's story, no one had yet seen Jesus.

How stunned the men would have been, had they known Jesus himself was the stranger with whom they were speaking and witnessing in His resurrection body! *"Then Jesus said to them, 'You foolish people! You find it so hard to believe all that the prophets wrote in the Scriptures. Wasn't it clearly predicted that the Messiah would have to suffer all these things before entering his glory?' Then Jesus took them through the writings of Moses and all the prophets, explaining from all the Scriptures the things concerning himself"* (Luke 24:25-27, NLT).

The two men invited the stranger to dine with them that evening. Jesus *"took bread, gave thanks, broke it, and began to give it to them. Then their eyes were opened and they recognized him"* (Luke 24:30-31). The identification of their Master was more than mental recall. Their eyes suddenly developed spiritual sight to discern what divine intervention had previously prevented them from acknowledging. Their hearts were suddenly on fire with the familiarity of their Master's characteristic love and divine authority.

When mortals interact with the immortal, a change of heart naturally occurs.

At the moment the men acknowledged Him, Jesus disappeared from their presence. Immediately the two men walked back to Jerusalem to announce to the eleven disciples that they had met the Savior following His resurrection. *"While they were still talking about this, Jesus himself stood among them and said to them, 'Peace be with you'" (Luke 24:36).*

Imagine the advantage of having a camera mounted inside the Emmaus Café to record body language, the utter wonder and amazement registered on the men's faces when they suddenly discerned Jesus' true identity. Or if Jesus had been equipped with a listening device in his tunic pocket, their entire conversation would have been captured for posterity.

But wait! There was no need for modern technology to preserve the interaction of the resurrected Savior and His devout followers. God has equipped us with his written Word filled with inspired dialogue. The Old Testament is interspersed with myriad prophecies promising a future Messiah. The Magi who followed the supernatural star in the east were apprised of a revelation that the King of the Jews would be born in Bethlehem (Micah 5:2). Centuries before Jesus' incarnation on earth, the prophet Isaiah accurately described the Savior's humble beginnings, His divine ministry, and His amazing triumph over sin and suffering as the Lamb of God (Isaiah 53).

Our heavenly Father is faithful; His integrity impeccable. What God promises, He delivers, even when a covenant is established millenniums in advance. Every detail is meticulously followed, with no last minute changes. Many prophesies have already come to pass, occurring exactly as the Lord specified. *"For everything that was written in the past was written to teach us, so that through the endurance taught in the Scriptures and the encouragement they provide, we might have hope" (Romans 15:4).*

With such numerous promises from Almighty God, we need only open our Bibles to access the prophecies assuring us of a marvelous future spent in heaven in the presence of our Savior. Although we anticipate the grandeur of heaven, worshipping our Savior face-to-face, we need not wait until the future to celebrate a daily walk with Jesus.

Consider the staggering reaction of Cleopas and his friend, whose downcast spirits were suddenly exalted to a pinnacle of emotional triumph when the truth of Jesus' identity was revealed. Take heart; God still promises unsurpassed victory to believers today. *"Everyone born of God overcomes the world. This is the victory that has overcome the world, even our faith" (1 John 5:4).* A new age of grace and mercy was initiated when Jesus died and arose for all. Each of God's plans for His Son, who willingly accepted His role in the salvation of mankind, were carried out as prophesied.

Do you respond to your Savior with wonder and amazement? Jesus is patiently waiting for you to seek Him at every opportunity. Follow the disciples' example, who upon learning of Jesus' true identity, prayed with Him, served Him, and witnessed to others that their Messiah lived. In light of Jesus' sacrifice and the fulfill-ment of His faithful, fabulous promises, how can we offer any less than our love and our lives for Him?

CPSIA information can be obtained
at www.ICGtesting.com
Printed in the USA
FSHW010230060220
66768FS